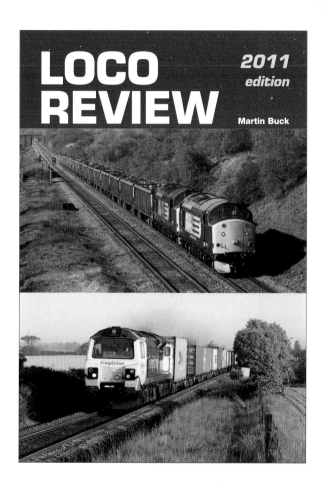

LOCO REVIEW

2011 *edition*

Martin Buck

FREIGHTMASTER

PUBLISHING

Contents

First published, November 2010, by:

Freightmaster Publishing
158 Overbrook
SWINDON
SN3 6AY

www.freightmasterpublishing.co.uk

Printed By:

Stephens & George
Goat Mill Road
Dowlais
MERTHYR TYDFIL
CF48 3TD

www.stephensandgeorge.co.uk

ISBN : 978-0-9558275-4-9

Cover Images : **Nigel Gibbs** *(top)* / **Nick Slocombe** *(bottom)*

Opposite : DRS Class 37s No37611 + 37059 double head 6M82, Coatbridge - Daventry, seen approaching Abington in the Upper Clyde Valley on 3rd June.   Guy Houston

Note : All dates in the text are 2010, unless otherwise stated.

Setting the Scene

Loco Review - 2011 follows on from where the previous edition left off with plenty more interesting loco-hauled activity and fantastic images to whet the appetite. This book is a 'window' of opportunity for photographers to show off their excellent photographic exploits - as in previous editions, the quality of images on offer is superb.

I am pleased to say that some new contributors have come on board to offer yet more variety and I am sure you will enjoy looking at their work as well. My thanks go to all the people named on the last page for their contributions without which this publication would definitely not exist. The majority of images have not been published before, although there is some replication, which is somewhat inevitable, but worthy of inclusion all the same.

In this edition there's lots to see and with several loco classes celebrating a 'Golden' Anniversary, there's an opportunity to dip into the archives for some 'golden' oldies. In particular, Peter Tandy has kindly submitted a portfolio of photographs to celebrate the Class 33 'Cromptons' and I have dipped into my small collection to pick out some Class 37s.

Of course, there is also the 'GWR 175' and this could not be allowed to slip through the net without some form of representation, however brief.

As for the loco scene, it is again the few which command the most attention, especially the diminishing Class 60 fleet; photographers seeking out their every move - petroleum flows being their best bet of finding work although other duties have thrown up a '60'.

When it comes to the DBS 37s, if it wasn't for No.37425 being despatched on ballast duties, there would be no activity at all. Colas Rail '47s' and '56s' continue to find work, whilst DRS '37s' & '57s' have been a welcome breath of fresh air on trains to Sheerness (scrap metal) and Daventry (intermodal) - heritage traction prevailing in an otherwise GM world!

The new 'Powerhaul' Class 70s enter revenue earning service and their popularity is mixed amongst enthusiasts - it seems one either likes them or hates them, with no middle ground! That said they have provided local interest with their initial breaking-in on Rugeley and Fiddlers Ferry coal trains, plus 70001's virtual dominance on Felixstowe - Lawley Street freightliners.

And, what can we look forward to ....

.... well, just for starters, we will follow the progress of the second batch of Class 70s to arrive in the UK and see what antics the new 'celebrity' Class 60 No.60099 gets up to, now in the colours of Indian steel giant Tata steel. This is very welcome, but who'd have thought DBS would spruce up another Class 60 at a time of cutbacks in the fleet.

So, enough said, please turn the page and see for yourself, the excitement and photographic opportunities loco-hauled freight and passenger turns have to offer today's enthusiast. Work starts now on the next edition of *LOCO REVIEW,* so get those cameras primed ready for action and send me your images. Enjoy!

Martin Buck

IT'S 'SNOW' JOKE

More Heavy Snow

Wow, who'd have thought it .... if the Winter of 2009 was bad enough, 2010 is even worse, bringing widespread disruption to rail services across the network during January and February 2010, well into April too, as far as Scotland is concerned!

Significant 'dumps' of snow fall across the country making travel a nightmare for both the travelling public and railway operating authorities, alike. However, for our intrepid photographers it's a challenge and, as ever and undaunted by the conditions, they set out once again to record the scene for you. Here is a selection of their work.

Above: *On 8th January, DBS Class 92 No.92017 'Bart The Engine' hurries south on the WCML at Euxton with the late running 4M48, Mossend - Rugby, fully laden 'Tesco Express' intermodal.* Fred Kerr

Opposite: *The snow lays deep and all around LED Signal No.7 at Crouch Hill, which is just about half way between Gospel Oak and South Tottenham on the 'GOBLIN.'* Nick Slocombe

---

'Upper Clyde Splendour'

(Overleaf)

Page 6: Wandel Mill - *DRS Class 66/4 No.66420 passes Wandel Mill, north of Abington, on 8th January hauling 4M44, the 08:47 Mossend - Daventry, running about 60 minutes late on an extremely cold day when there was much disruption. This train previously carried Stobart boxes and, this being the first week when DB Schenker operate the Stobart traffic, is the reason for the empty wagons. This train is withdrawn a few weeks later.*

Donald Cameron

Page 7: Crawford - *Now in the hands of a 'Shed', Class 66/0 No.66114 has the honours on the morning of 12th January working 6S36, Dalston - Grangemouth, empty petroleum, formed of the distinctive and easily-recognisable green-liveried TEA bogie tanks. The train is seen crossing Lamington Viaduct, on a day when one can almost feel the icy cold waters of the infant River Clyde below.* Alastair Blackwood

West Highland Mail .... *well, not quite! A stunning image where the train is dwarfed by the majestic snow-clad peaks of Beinn Mhanach and Beinn Heasgarnich. GBRf Class 66/7 No.66728 'Institution of Railway Operators' (above) is making its way round the mass of Beinn Dorain hauling two Royal Mail Class 325 EMU sets as a load for route learning in preparation for taking over the Alcan traffic from DBS.*   Alastair Blackwood

Icy Tayside .... *truly magical, even though there is not a train to be seen! The clouds cast fine reflections on the Firth of Tay where lumps of ice can be seen floating on the surface. The Tay railway bridge (below) dominates the image, approximately two and a quarter miles in length, which links Dundee and Wormit.*   Jim Ramsay

Still the Snow Lingers .... *although the snow clears (temporarily) from the lowlands, copious amounts still linger on the Scottish mountains dominating the skyline to the north of Stirling - in fact, heavy downfalls of snow were still disrupting rail traffic well into April. On 9th February, Class 66/5 No.66548 (above) passes Braehead in the southern outskirts of Stirling with 4C07, the 13:26 Longannet - Ravenstruther, HYA empties.* Alastair Blackwood

A striking view of Class 92 No.92031 'The Institute of Logistics and Transport' (below) topping Beattock Summit (1,016ft above sea level) on 2nd April, working 6S51, Carlisle Yard - Mossend, departmental service comprising 10 side tipping ballast wagons and two sets of autoballasters. Keith McGovern

'Double Docker'

On 8th January, the photographer braves the elements and makes his way across the Pennines to Docker, where he is rewarded with a cloudless winter sky and some stunning images. 'Constellation' Class 86/7, No.86702 'Cassiopeia' + 3 Class 325 units (above) sweep past Docker on an additional 1Z96, Shieldmuir - Warrington, laid on to help clear a backlog of mail, which had built up due to the bad weather hindering collections and deliveries.

As the sun begins to dip below the Fells and the shadows lengthen, DRS Compass-liveried Class 57 No.57003 (below) rushes south in charge of 6J37, Carlisle Yard - Chirk, loaded timber. Two months later Colas Rail Class 66/8s start working this train, No.66843 in particular. Richard Armstrong (2)

Keep The Home Fires Burning

During extremely cold weather, power stations work overtime to keep the nation supplied with heat and power, consuming vast tonnages of coal in the process. On 9th January, Metronet-liveried Class 66/7 No.66721 (above) 'Harry Beck' hurries through Eagle Lane, Knottingley, with 6H93, the 07:35 Tyne Dock - Drax, loaded GBRf coal working while, in the background, Ferrybridge power station does it's bit towards global warming!   Ian Ball

Meanwhile, as a blizzard rages, Class 66/3 No.66305 (below) passes the Lafarge stone terminal at Grimsbury, Banbury, on 6th January working 6Z37, the 09:23 Daw Mill - Didcot.   Nigel Gibbs

In the West ....

On 7th January, unbranded ATW Class 57/3, No.57316 (above), top 'n' tails No.57315 'The Mole' on 2U14, the 11:02 Taunton - Cardiff Central, running 105-minutes late when it is seen passing Magor on the South Wales Main Line; the consist includes three former Anglia Railways Mk2 vehicles on this occasion.   Jamie Squibbs

Following an overnight covering of snow, Class 66/0 No.66124 (below) passes Norton Bavant on 7th January with a late running 6O41, Westbury - Eastleigh engineers train, formed of Network Rail JNA Bogie Ballast wagons, full of spoil on this occasion.   Kevin Poole

.... In the East

From December 2009 right through to March 2010, most of the country did not escape heavy snowfall, like in the low-lying Fenland. On 19th December 2009, an unidentified DBS Class 66/0 (above) loco heads away from the camera at Middle Road Crossing, March, with a rake of 2-axle PAA covered sand hoppers, forming the previous day's 6E84, Middleton Towers - Barnby Dun, sand train. Nick Slocombe

On the same day, Gresley Pacific 4-6-2 No.60007 'Sir Nigel Gresley' (above) approaches Peterborough station, heading 1Z21, the 06:48 London King's Cross - Newcastle, 'Christmas Tynesider'; the early morning sun giving a pleasing golden glint on the coaches .... **is anywhere free of snow?** Jamie Squibbs

Two for the price of one on 7th January .... as luck would have it, Class 66/5 No.66569 (above) heads across Bishton Flyover with 4O51, Wentloog - Southampton, freightliner running 70 minutes late, just as an unidentified HST passes below on the main line en-route to London Paddington.

Jamie Squibbs

On the East Lancs Railway, Class 40 No.40145 'East Lancashire Railway' + Class 37/4 No.37418 'Pectinidae' (below) double head 2J62, the 11:30 Rawtenstall - Heywood on 9th January, as they climb through Heap Bridge. How much longer will it be before the 'Whistler' reverts back to BR Blue livery?

Neil Harvey

14

4th January 2010 marks the start of D B Schenker (DBS) operating the Scottish 'Stobart' train from Mossend to Inverness, having taken over running this traffic from Direct Rail Services (DRS). However, it proves to be an inauspicious start!

The northbound service - 4H47, Mossend to Inverness - arrives some two hours late in the Highland Capital due to a points problem at Mossend but, as the rest of the day proves, it is better to be late than sorry ....

on the return in heavy snow, 4N47, the 13:14 Inverness - Mossend, derails at Carrbridge behind Class 66/0 No.66048 with a consist of ten FKA wagons loaded with empty containers.

Network Rail confirm the train passed Signal AC336 at danger before being derailed on trap points at the north end of the station; the loco and next two vehicles coming to rest down an embankment with the following four vehicles straddled across the lines. Fortunately, there are no fatalities.

At the time, there is no apparent reason for the crash although it may have been the case that a build-up of ice on the wagons caused brake failure resulting in the driver being unable to stop the train. It is worth noting that temperatures in Scotland had been recorded as low as -15 deg C and 4N47 was in the process of making the 4-mile descent from Slochd Summit (ruling gradient of 1 in 60) to Carrbridge, travelling at around 55mph when the driver started to apply the brakes.

4H47

The first run of the DBS 'Stobart' train .... No.66048 (above) arrives safely at Inverness on 4th January with suitably branded 'Curtainside' FKAs, running as 4H47, Mossend - Inverness.   Steven Robertson

A road snowplough is brought in before the clear-up could start and DBS Class 37/4 No.37425 is despatched to take the four wagons not derailed back to Inverness. The '37' had been on hire to Network Rail in Scotland for snow patrol duties.

The Highland Line reopens to traffic on 12th January, prior to which freight services are diverted via Aberdeen.

No.66048 *'James the Engine'*, having just been repainted at Toton TMD in 'Stobart Rail' colours, remains at Carrbridge until mid-February, when it is finally lifted from the woods that have been its home for 6 weeks; trees and shrubbery being cleared to facilitate the move.

4N47

No.66048 'James the Engine' (above) sets off from Inverness near Cradlehall working the ill fated 4N47, Inverness - Mossend, 'Stobart' intermodal on behalf of Tesco. An hour after this picture was taken the train derails & crashes down an embankment at Carrbridge.   Steven Robertson

This is the final resting place for No.66048 (below) at the bottom of the embankment.   Jim Ramsay

DRS go for Scrap

Following the demise of Advenza last October, DRS take on the former operator's scrap metal services. Malcolm-branded Class 66/4 No.66412 (above) is running 60-minutes late as it dodges the shadows at Burton Salmon on 28th January, while in charge of the Thursday only 6Z66, Stockton - Shipley scrap. The consist is formed JXA, former Sheerness Co-Steel, bogie scrap wagons. Richard Armstrong

A new long distance flow (6Z90, Tyne Dock - Sheerness) sees scrap metal moved to the steelworks on the Isle of Sheppey. On a dismal 12th March, No.66431 (below) is seen on the return journey (6Z70, Sheerness - Tyne Dock), passing South Darenth, just east of Farningham Road station. See later for 37s on 6Z90! Alan Hazelden

6X88, Hartlepool - Georgemas Junction

July sees the start of a weekly flow bringing (large) pipes from Hartlepool Steelworks to the far North of Scotland, destined for the Wester Oil pipeline fabrication yard in Wick. The flow is believed to run for 40 weeks. After an extended stop at Perth, No.66101 (below) approaches Charleston Crossing, Murthly (Highland Line) on 13th July with 6X88 Hartlepool - Georgemas Junction. Due to the length of the pipes, 2-axle (RRA) wagons (below) are used to accommodate the overhanging section of pipes.   Jim Ramsay (2)

> **Mar sin leibh DBS / Hallo agus fàilte GBRf**

22nd February

One of the longest running Anglo-Scottish DBS (formerly EWS) flows goes over to GBRf operation - the *Alcan* (Rio Tinto) alumina traffic between Fort William and Lynemouth.

The service:

6S44, 11:30 North Blyth - Fort William   6E45, 15:15 Fort William - North Blyth

Local 'Trips':

6N58, North Blyth - Lynemouth   6N51, Lynemouth - North Blyth

6N69, North Blyth - Lynemouth   6N32, Lynemouth - North Blyth

Route Learning

On Saturday, 13th February, route learning takes place on the West Highland Line as GBRf run Class 66/7 No.66728 *'Institution of Railway Operators'* with two Royal Mail Class 325 EMU sets as a load for route learning, in preparation for taking over the Alcan traffic.

Background

Aluminium is produced from Aluminium Oxide (Alumina), a constituent of Bauxite ore. The British Aluminium (now Alcan) smelter at Lochaber, Fort William, opened in 1929 and, following modernisation in the 1980's, started to receive imported alumina from North Blyth, using former grain hoppers, before handing over to PCA 2-axle tanks. In North East England, another smelter was opened at Lynemouth in 1971, close to the Port of Blyth, where the imported alumina would arrive.

For many years, the finished product (Aluminium ingots) was transported by rail from both smelters using Freightliner services, running to Cardiff Pengam before the traffic switched to EWS. Unfortunately, all ingot traffic is now conveyed by road; the last dedicated service ceasing in Summer 2009; ingots 'tripped' from Lynemouth to Tees Yard to form 6V49, Tees - Newport Docks.

'Alcan' Portfolio

The new order - GBRf Class 66/7 No.66726 (above) is seen passing County March summit (1,024ft above sea level) with the return Alumina empties on 19th June, running as 6Y45, Fort William - Braidhurst Loop, Hamilton. No.66726 is one of the 66/7s named after a football club, in this case 'Sheffield Wednesday'.   David Stracey

As a prelude to the contract starting, GBRf schedule a 'one off' driver training run over the weekend of 13th / 14th February. The unlikely, and probably 'never to be repeated', combination of a Class 66/7 No.66728 and two Class 325 Royal Mail EMUs form this train - no PCAs being available. The 325s (spare all weekend) are ideal as they are built to the same gauge as Class 150 type DMUs. The train is seen (opposite) traversing Horse Shoe Curve viaduct.   Alastair Blackwood

The last trainload of Alumina (6S44) to run under the auspices of DBS is hauled by No.66110 on 19th February. After depositing the loaded PCAs, No.66110 (below) is seen running light to the nearby depot, before returning south with the final DBS Alcan service to Tyne Yard (see Page 22).   Jim Ramsay

(OVERLEAF)

Page 22: *Last rites .... a stunning view showing off the magnificent West Highland scenery to the full with the olny hint of civilisation being a solitary electricity pylon. This is the last DBS operated Alcan service (6Y15, Mossend - Fort William); No.66110 has the honour and is approaching Achallader on Friday, 19th February.* Jim Ramsay

Page 23: *A superb close up view of No.66725 'Sunderland' descending across the viaduct to Rannoch station on 22nd February with empty Alumina tanks, forming 6E45, Fort William - North Blyth.*

Alastair Blackwood

December 2009 is a sad month on Teesside as steelmaker Corus confirm it will curtail production at its Teesside Cast Products factory, putting 1,700 people out of work. It had been confirmed in May that the 150-year-old Redcar plant was to be mothballed.

The plant had been at risk since a 10-year deal suddenly fell through, which was signed by an international consortium, led by Italian steel specialists Marcegaglia in 2004, committing the consortium to buy around 78% of the Redcar plant's production.

Redcar is partially mothballed at the end of January, shutting its blast furnace, its steel melt shop - which makes slab - and one of the two coke ovens. It will be keeping open the wharf facility that handles imports and shipping, the other coke oven and some of the power generation capacity. The company said operating a merchant slab plant with output of three million tonnes a year was "not sustainable" without a long-term partner.

A consequence of this news means the end of an iconic freight flow on Teesside, limestone from Hardendale using the unique HGA and CBA 'White Lady' 2-axle wagons:

> 6E46, Hardendale Quarry - Redcar   6M46, Redcar - Hardendale

A further consequence is the removal of surplus stocks of Iron Ore from Redcar for use at Scunthorpe steelworks using JTA / JUA tipplers off the Immingham - Santon circuit, which are spare on a Saturday. There are three STP flows:

> 6N01, FO 23:45 Immingham - Redcar   6D01, SO 06:30 Redcar - Santon
> 6N02, SO 02:05 Santon - Redcar   6D02, SO 09:15 Redcar - Santon
> 6Z03, SO 03:40 Santon - Redcar   6D03, SO 11:34 Redcar - Santon

In addition, some of the above trains will not be carrying Iron Ore, but a by-product of the smelting process - 'Furnace Burden' - which looks like limestone and is a combination of limestone, coke and ore, which will also be going to Scunthorpe.

Trainloads of redundant Iron Ore and Limestone-like 'Furnace Burden' are being moved from Redcar to Scunthorpe steelworks. In this view, Class 60 No.60096 (opposite) heads along the ECML at Newsham, Thirsk, on 13th March with the third train of the day, running as 6A03, the 11:34 (SO) Redcar - Santon, and a payload of 'Furnace Burden'.   Ian Ball

Here is a reminder of the daily Limestone train to / from Hardendale Quarry. On 4th April 2009, No.66020 (below) is the motive power for 6M46, Rodcar - Hardendale, seen hard at work on the last few miles of its journey from Teesside, passing Little Strickland (Thrimby). The consist is made up of three distinctive sections: CBAs, HGAs, plus some containerised lime FCAs at the rear of the train.

                              Ian Ball

The two types of wagon used to convey Limestone to Redcar (and Lackenby) are unique in their design: the CBA 2-axle Covered Hopper and HGA 2-axle Limestone Hopper, both illustrated on this page.

CBA No.362162 (top right).
HGA No.362094 (centre).

The locations are Tees Yard and Thornaby, respectively, both in the consist of 6M46, Redcar - Hardendale.

                       Martin Buck (2)

On 25th March, rail maintenance company Jarvis announce it will go into administration after lenders refuse to offer the Company further credit. As a result of big reductions in its business since the beginning of the recession in 2008, creditors are not prepared to offer the money needed for the business to continue as a going concern. Jarvis have no option but to go into administration and suspend trading in its shares.

This decision also affects its railfreight subsidiary, Fastline, who operate coal flows to Radcliffe power station on behalf of power generator eON, with coal sourced from Daw Mill, Hatfield and Liverpool BIT. When Fastline cease operations on 31st March, eON approach Freightliner Heavy Haul to take over the Ratcliffe flow and a new daily diagram is set up:

```
4G53, 23:27  Hunslet - Daw Mill
6A53, 08:50  Daw Mill - Ratcliffe
4G13, 13:30  Ratcliffe - Barrow Hill

4E59, 06:00  Ratcliffe - Hatfield Mine
6A59, 12:02  Hatfield - Ratcliffe
4G43, 17:20  Ratcliffe - Daw Mill
6E86, 01:00  Daw Mill - Ratcliffe

6M66, 03:49  Immingham - Rugeley
4G92, 12:15  Rugeley - Daw Mill
6E05, 17:07  Daw Mill - Ratcliffe
4E84, 23:05  Ratcliffe - Barrow Hill
```

Administration means that more than 2,000 Jarvis employee's jobs are at risk and Fastline's fleet of Class 66/3s and rolling stock will be placed in store.

Fastline in operation .... Class 66/3 No.66303 (above) passes Hatton & Tutbury on the seldom photographed Stoke-on-Trent to Derby main line with 6Z30, Liverpool Bulk Terminal - Ratcliffe power station. Running on 19th March, the train goes via North Staffordshire Jct, Stenson Jct and Sheet Stores Jct to reach the power station.

As a consequence of administration, the leased Fastline IIAs and hired-in HYAs have to go back and several wagon moves take place to facilitate this. On 3rd April, Colas Rail Class 47/7 No.47727 'Rebecca' (above) is used to take some IIAs to Gloucester and the train (6Z48, ex Chaddesden) is seen passing Hargate.

Surely, a candidate for working of the year! With GBRf eager to get back its assets, two Harry Needle Railway Company Class 20/9 locos, Nos.20901 and 20905, (overleaf) pass Sutton Bonnington on 26th March with 6Z22, Chaddesden - Peterborough, stock move of hired-in GBRf HYA bogie coal hoppers.   Mick Tindall (3)

Viewed from Stainforth East UWC on 8th April, the driver and a shunter look over some paper work as low emission Class 66/9 No.66951 (below) waits for the over head bunker to refill with coal to allow the rest of the train to re-load. The train will then leave with 6A59, the 12:02 Hatfield Colliery - Ratcliffe, formed of 20 loaded HXA hoppers full of black Yorkshire gold from the Barnsley seam.   James Skoyles

After a year or so from being absent from the rail network, the GBRf operated 'Mud Oil' train from Harwich to Aberdeen resumes with a Class 66/7 loco hauling a rake of Carless TTA 2-axle tank wagons. 'Mud oil' is actually a drilling fluid for use in the North Sea oil industry.

Although the same loco will work the train throughout, due to the length of the journey, the run comprises separate sections, thus:

    6E06, FO   19:15 Harwich - Peterborough Yard
    6D60, MO 06:05 Peterborough Yard - Doncaster Decoy
    6S60, TO   07:08 Doncaster Decoy - Aberdeen Waterloo

    6E59, ThO 06:25 Aberdeen Waterloo - Doncaster Decoy
    6L59, FO   16:24 Doncaster Decoy - Harwich

It is pleasing to report the return of the 'Mud Oil' train (6S60) from Harwich to Aberdeen as it has been missing from the rail network for well over 12-months. On 4th March, Class 66/7 No.66725 'Sunderland' (above) is heading south at Newton Hall, Durham, with the 6E59 empties returning to Harwich. This was supposed to work the previous week, but became delayed due to inclement weather in Scotland.   Carl Gorse

Earlier in the day, this attractive composition captures No.66725 (previous page) on 6E59, running along the banks of the Firth of Forth at Burntisland 'on time' at 10:00hrs. This is the first leg of the long journey back to East Anglia - 6E59, the 06:25 Aberdeen Waterloo - Doncaster 'Down' Decoy yard.   David Hamilton

---------------------------------- ~ ------------------------------------

Flyash

6M45, Drax - Earles

A recent addition to the freight timetable is 6M45, a trainload of Flyash from Drax to Earles, which is used in the production of cement to reduce the carbon footprint. On 2nd March, Class 66/6 No.66606 (top right) is heading out of Knottingley with 6E45, (TO) Earles - Drax, empty Flyash tanks. The skyline is dominated by the cooling towers of Ferrybridge power station.   Richard Armstrong

6Z45, Drax - Aberthaw

A 'STP' weekly flow of flyash from Drax to Aberthaw starts in mid May. Here, running as 6Z45, the 12:08 MO Crewe Basford Hall - Aberthaw, No.66622 (bottom right) passes Dorrington on 24th May, where the once pleasant view has been dramatically changed due to intrusive pallisade fencing and other paraphernalia.   Mike Hemming

Aggregate

A new flow starts on the Cumbrian Coast line, albeit STP, but non-nuclear .... the movement of stone for a building project near Millom, conveyed in JNAs as 6C36, Workington Docks - Drigg. On 16th April, the train is seen (above) passing Derwent Junction, top 'n' tailed by Nos.66427 and 66423 for operational purposes.   Ian Ball

Although railfreight associated with the Port of Avonmouth is mostly coal, there is the occasional flow of imported stone to Westbury and / or Acton. On 10th April, MendipRail Class 59/1 No.59103 'Village of Mells' (below) slowly hauls 15 loaded JNAs up the graded 'freight only' line from Hallen Marsh to Stoke Gifford, forming 6C64, the 14:10 (ThO) Avonmouth Bennetts - Westbury. This striking vantage point looking across the M5 Motorway to the River Severn is near the hamlet of Blaise, Bristol.   Dave Gower

Cement

Although 'mothballed' for cement production, Westbury cement works is handling a weekly trainload of cement from Earles for onward distribution. On 23rd April, No.66611 (above) is on a rake of empty JPAs, running as 6M37, Westbury - Earles, and is passing Pilning, having been routed via Severn Tunnel. DBS Class 66/0 No.66037 on 6B35, Hayes - Moreton on Lugg, is stuck in the 'Down' Goods Loop, due to a points problem. Dave Gower

Any new freight flow over the 'Copy Pit' route between Burnley and Todmorden is worthy of note. After finishing duties on the Ketton - St.Pancras flow, a rake of 'Castle Cement' PCA 2-axle tanks make their way to the cement works at Horrocksford, Clitheroe, to work a loaded train to Leicester. With Burnley and Pendle Hill prominent in the background, No.66003 (below) lugs 6Z73, the 13:50 (SO) Clitheroe - Leicester, towards Copy Pit Summit at Walk Mill, near Cliviger on 26th June. Neil Harvey

Bigger Role for Didcot

DB Schenker undertake a 'General Freight Review' to make the Wagonload sector more streamlined and cost-efficient with the resultant changes in freight flows taking effect from March 2010 onwards. Basically, 'marginal' and 'less than trainload' flows have been kept, but amalgamated to be more economical.

DBS create a new Network, based on the profitable MoD and Automotive trunk flows, with other wagonload traffic being accommodated on the new network or moved to trainload operation. The new Wagonload and Automotive network is based around Didcot and Warrington and these are the main aspects of the 'General Freight Review':

1. Wembley yard closes

2. Car traffic transfers from Bescot to Warrington

3. Didcot

Already a major MoD 'hub', Didcot now has an enhanced role for Wagonload services and here are some of the new workings:

6M11,	WFO	07:12	Didcot yard - Blechley 'Cemex'	Lime Mortar tanks
6V90,	FO	04:17	Dollands Moor - Didcot yard	Wagonload
6X48,		14:29	Dagenham - Didcot yard	Ford cars
6V11,	WFO	14:30	Blechley 'Cemex' - Didcot yard	Empty Lime Mortar tanks
6O89,	WO	21:26	Didcot yard - Dollands Moor	Wagonload
6V31,		19:48	Dagenham - Didcot yard	Wagonload
6L31,		01:10	Didcot yard - Dagenham	Wagonload
6V60,	WO	22:39	(Tue) Dollands Moor - Didcot yard	Wagonload
6L35,		04:49	Didcot yard - Dagenham	Empty car carriers

No.66116 (above) passes Dullingham on 21st June with 6R34, Ipswich - Ripple Lane, Wagonload service conveying vans from Ely and fuel oil tanks from Ipswich. This is a new (Wednesday Only) working resulting from the Wagonload 'Review' and is the only freight booked over the single line Chippenham Junction - Newmarket - Coldham Lane Junction, Cambridge route. David Stracey

Didcot *'Wagonload'* Variety

One completely new flow to the Great Western Main Line is the twice-weekly flow of Lime Mortar powder from Peak Forest to the Cemex terminal at Bletchley, conveyed in distinctive orange liveried ex-RMC 2-axle PCA tank wagons. Here, No.66132 (above) is nearing journey's end with 6V11, Bletchley - Didcot, PCA empties; wagons which used to travel to Bletchley direct from Peak Forest.

A cracking freight, in terms of consist; 6X48, Dagenham - Didcot, Ford cars....

On 22nd June, the train is fully loaded with at least four varieties of car transporters in tow as No.66090 (below) slows for a signal check at Didcot East Junction. Martin Buck (2)

This elevated view shows the site of the new freightliner terminal and its location in relation to the Taunton - Bristol main line. On 11th August, Freightliner Class 66/5 No.66576 (above) pulls out of the terminal with a train of empty containers, forming 4L32, Bristol FLT - Tilbury.

The lines to the right of the loco lead to Portbury Dock, which is used by DBS and FHH respectively, to move imported cars to Mossend and imported coal to Rugeley power station. The line is only double track for nine chains between Parson Street Junction and Ashton Junction, thence single track continues for the remaining eight miles to the end of the line. Dave Gower

Bristol Freightliner Terminal Re-opens

A new freightliner terminal opens in July near Parson Street, Bristol, on the site of the old freightliner terminal, which closed more than 20-years ago - remember the Class 46-hauled Bristol - Follingsby (Newcastle) freightliner?

Liquid logistics company Trans Ocean win a three year contract to import wines into the UK for Constellation Europe, transporting bulk and cased wines from Europe and the New World into Constellation's wine facility in Avonmouth, the largest in Europe. Constellation makes brands such as Hardy's and Banrock Station.

The re-opening of the rail link and the depot means wine can be shipped directly from the South East ferry ports, rather than driven across the country by lorry, thus eliminating 10,000 journeys and 1 million road miles each year. Under a joint scheme operated by Network Rail and Freightliner, seven trains packed with booze will rumble into the terminal every week.

The reporting details of the new services are as follows, the origination point of entry into the UK is dependent on where the ship will berth:

4V30,	23:00	Tilbury - Bristol FLT	4L32,	11:00	Bristol FLT - Tilbury
4V26,	23:10	Thamesport - Bristol FLT	4O24,	11:00	Bristol FLT - Thamesport
4V32,	11:11	Ipswich Yard - Bristol FLT	4L30,	10:00	Bristol FLT - Felixstowe

DRS Launch New Initiative

DRS, one of the UK's leading rail freight operators, start trials to move freight from the East Coast to the West Coast using a new type of wagon to enable a cross country service to operate with the necessary gauge clearance.

These trials use a DRS Class 66 on behalf of P&O Ferrymasters, a Company that continuously seeks to provide customers with sustainable solutions using intermodal products. The trials form part of a project by DRS that looks at ways of accommodating the increasingly popular high-cube ISO containers within the British loading gauge.

A two week trial starts on 19th July, the initial phase moving freight using a traditional 'Megafret' wagon carrying a 9ft 6ins container. Due to restricted gauge clearance on some of the lines the route from Teesport to Widnes is via Edinburgh, Carlisle and Crewe.

Phase 2 begins on 26th July, using an innovative IDA 'Lowliner' wagon to move the container. 'Lowliner' wagons are particularly useful for conveying high-cube containers where the loading gauge may vary on the route. This train crosses the country from Teesport to Widnes via Derby and Crewe and demonstrates service efficiency as well as reducing journey times. A regular service is scheduled for September but, initially:

4Z58, MWFO 18:30 Tees Dock - Ditton   4Z60, TThO 20:59 Ditton - Tees Dock

4Z58, Tees Dock - Ditton

Super power for a light load .... instead of a DRS Class 66/4 loco, Class 37/0 locos No.37087 + No.37229 (above) are chosen to work this particular intermodal trial on 30th July. Originally, a change of driver is scheduled for Derby but there is a last minute change to Burton-on-Trent, resulting in the relief driver being 30 minutes late - long enough for a time exposure shot to be had there of 4Z58, Tees Dock - Ditton.

The two '37s' are named 'Keighley & Worth Valley 40th Anniversary 1968 - 2008' *and* 'Jonty Jarvis 8-12-1998 to 18-3-2005', *respectively.*   Mick Tindall

On 25th March, Colas Class 66/8 No.66843 (above) leaves Hellifield with 6J37, the 12:29 Carlisle Yard - Chirk, loaded timber for Kronospan. The train is heading for Blackburn on the Hellifield - Daisyfield Junction line, which is ostensibly 'freight only', but is an important diversionary route when engineering work takes place on the WCML between Preston and Carlisle. The line does have photographic potential but, as daytime freight traffic is few and far between, this probably explains why the line does not attract much photographic activity. Neil Harvey

Colas Rail have the responsibility of moving timber on behalf of Kronsopan from Carlisle Yard to Chirk and employ their own distinctive liveried Class 66/8s on these trains:

      6J37, 12:29 Carlisle Yard - Chirk   6C37, 22:25 Chirk - Carlisle Yard

These trains are routed via the WCML although they also travel via the Settle & Carlisle on occasions. The timber is carried in converted 'Cargowaggons':

Design Code   : KF056A

Carkind   : KFA

The wagons in the 'Pool' are all prefixed GERS and numbered:

97106	97109	97112	97126	97138	97147	97148	97151	97153	97158	97161
97162	97166	97168	97170	97171	97211	97214	97216	97220	97221	97229
97233	97235	97247	97266	97268	97276	97309				

From August, Colas secure another contract from Kronsopan, this time moving timber from a loading point at Ribblehead to Chirk; the empty timber carriers moving to the site from Carlisle Upperby, via WCML or Settle & Carlisle and reversal at Hellifield.

The diagram is:

      6Z41,   14:15 Carlisle - Ribblehead
      6Z41, FO 19:05 Ribblehead - Chirk   6Z42, SO 13:58 Chirk - Ribblehead

This new service is allocated a single Colas Class 47 and once the timber carriers have arrived at Ribblehead, the '47' runs light engine (0Z41) to Crewe, returning when the timber has been loaded.

With blackening clouds dominating the 'Three Peaks', the photographer makes a good decision on 14th September to stay away from the drama and capture No.47739 'Robin of Templecombe' (above) rounding the curve at Long Preston, in a very lucky patch of sunshine. Whilst in charge of the late running 6Z41, Carlisle Upperby - Ribblehead, empty logs, the '47' is travelling to Hellifield to run round before heading back to the 'S. & C' and Ribblehead.

The loaded train does not leave Ribblehead until after seven o'clock in the evening which makes photographing this train rather difficult in the fading autumnal light. However, on 3rd September, No.47739 (below) is seen again, this time having left the loading site and across Batty Moss viaduct, heading for Blea Moor to run round. The train will then head south to Hellifield and take the Blackburn line, thence Farington Junction, WCML to Warrington, Chester and Wrexham. Richard Armstrong (2)

July sees GBRf move into Hunterston for the first time, operating a new flow of imported coal from the Bulk Import Terminal on the Ayrshire coast to Drax power station. The train is routed via the ex-GSWR, Tyne Valley and ECML on the outward journey, returning via the Settle & Carlisle. The reporting details are:

6H51, 18:21 Hunterston - Drax   4S51, 07:45 Drax - Hunterston

GBRf's Class 66/7 No.66707 'Valour ....' (top) is seen on the slog up from Hunterston (which can be seen in the background) towards West Kilbride on 24th August with 6H51, the 18:21 Hunterston - Drax. The train is travelling along the unelectrified 'Up' freight line, which is adjacent to the 'Up and Down' Largs line, which is electrified and used by Class 318 and 344 EMUs, running between Glasgow Central and Largs. Max Fowler

Returning to Scotland with the empty HYAs, No.66716 (above) heads north over Ribblehead Viaduct with 4S51, the 07:45 Drax - Hunterston, on a rather dull and overcast 18th August. Neil Harvey

Cardiff - Paignton

2U02, 06:19 Bristol T. M. - Cardiff Central
2C67, 08:00 Cardiff Central - Paignton
2U20, 12:47 Paignton - Cardiff Central
2C85, 17:00 Cardiff Central - Taunton
2M68, 19:18 Taunton - Bristol T. M.

Cardiff - Taunton

2D04, 07:28 Taunton - Bristol Parkway
2Y10, 09:13 Bristol Parkway - Weston - s - Mare
5U14, 10:09 Weston - s - Mare - Taunton
2U14, 11:02 Taunton - Cardiff Central
2C79, 14:00 Cardiff Central - Taunton
2U24, 16:16 Taunton - Cardiff Central
2C89, 19:00 Cardiff Central - Taunton

More of the same! FGW introduce a new Cardiff - Paignton diagram, effective from the December 2009 timetable change. Due to a continuing shortage of units, a rake of Mk2 air-conditioned coaches, top 'n' tailed by DBS Class 67s, are allocated to the diagram.

Consequently, the existing Cardiff - Taunton service starts off with hired-in Mk2 'air-cons' and hired-in Class 57s working in top 'n' tail formation. Interestingly, the '57s' and stock stable at Bishops Lydeard (West Somerset Railway) each weekday night, except on Friday.

On 10th February, the new Cardiff - Paignton service is a real 'Royal' occasion with No.67006 'Royal Sovereign' (leading) (top right) and No.67005 'Queen's Messenger' (tailing) in charge of 2C67, the 08:00 Cardiff Central – Paignton, which is seen passing Hollicombe.

Meanwhile, on 8th March, a pair of ordinary EWS-liveried Class 67s -No.67017 & No.67022 (above) - top 'n' tail 2U20, the 12:47 Paignton – Cardiff Central, photographed skirting the banks of the River Teign near Bishopsteignton, as seen from the south side of the river.   Robert Sherwood (2)

FGW **Cardiff - Taunton Portfolio**

Under GBRf **Control:** *Class 66/7 No.66721 'Harry Beck' (above) becomes the first non-Class '57' loco to work a FGW diagram. Due to consecutive failures, Class 57/3 No.57304 'Gordon Tracy' is replaced by No.66721 on 17th June, and is seen leading 2C79, the 14:00 Cardiff - Taunton, at Bishton on the South Wales main Line, top 'n' tailed with No.57305 'John Tracy'. No.66721 was commandeered at Taunton after working 4V11, Peterborough - Fairwater Yard.* Jamie Squibbs

On 28th June, 2C79 is depicted again, but with ex-DRS Class 66/4 (below) seen hauling the train along the single line section towards Weston-super-Mare; Class 57/3 No.57308 'Tin Tin' is 'Dead' on the rear. This proves to be the last week of operation by GBRF due to the high failure rate of the Class 57s. Chris Perkins

DBS Takeover: *It's 5th July and the first day of DBS operation. Class 67 No.67029 'Royal Diamond' (top right) brings up the rear of 2Y10, the 09.13 Bristol Parkway - Weston-super-Mare, as No.67018 'Keith Heller' heads away from Weston Milton. The consist comprises Mk2 vehicles Nos.9526, 5769, 5792 & 5748.* Chris Perkins

After hauling 2U02, the 06:19 Bristol Temple Meads - Cardiff Central on 13th May, No.67022 is now tailing 2C67, the 08:00 Cardiff Central - Paignton; No.67018 'Keith Heller (bottom right) is now the train engine and approaches Weston-super-Mare on the Worle Junction - Uphill Junction single line section. Steven King

↑ 67029 *'Royal Diamond'*   **67018** *'Keith Heller'* **▼**

22nd November 2009: Two road bridges spanning the River Derwent in Workington collapse due the heaviest rainfall in Cumbria since records began. The collapse of both the Northside bridge and Calva bridge have effectively cut Workington in half and results in a three-hour journey for people in the town to get from one side of the river to the other.

Due to the damaged roads and bridges, the disruption sees unprecedented demand for local rail services. To help Network Rail build a temporary station at Workington North to aid people wishing to commute across the river. The new station is built in six days on wasteland and features two platforms, a portable waiting room, a gravel car park and a footbridge.

A temporary, free, timetable service is introduced on Monday, 30th November 2009, whereby Direct Rail Services (DRS), working with Northern Rail, provide additional capacity between Maryport - Flimby - Workington North - Workington, utilising a rake of four air-conditioned Mk2 vehicles and DRS locos operating in top 'n' tail formation. The service is funded by the Department of Transport until 28th May, viz:

5Z20	05:45	Kingmoor - Workington	2T18	07:05	Workington - Maryport
2Z19	07:25	Maryport - Workington	2T20	08:10	Workington - Maryport
2Z21	08:33	Maryport - Workington	2T22	09:40	Workington - Maryport
2Z23	10:02	Maryport - Workington	2T24	10:30	Workington - Maryport
2Z25	10:50	Maryport - Workington	2T26	11:20	Workington - Maryport
2Z27	11:45	Maryport - Workington	2T28	12:20	Workington - Maryport
2Z29	12:50	Maryport - Workington	2T30	13:35	Workington - Maryport
2Z31	14:00	Maryport - Workington	2T32	14:45	Workington - Maryport
2Z33	15:10	Maryport - Workington	2T34	15:50	Workington - Maryport
2Z35	16:25	Maryport - Workington	2T36	17:00	Workington - Maryport
2Z37	18:10	Maryport - Workington	2T38	17:55	Workington - Maryport
2Z39	18:20	Maryport - Workington	2T40	18:50	Workington - Maryport
2Z41	19:15	Maryport - Workington	5Z21	20:35	Workington - Kingmoor

Top: *Looking back to the temporary Workington North station, No.47832 'Solway Princess' (top) and No.37423 'Spirit of The Lakes' (tail) pass Derwent junction with 2Z25, the 10:50 Maryport - Workington.* Ian Ball

This imposing head-on view features Class 37/6 No.37610 'TS (Ted) Cassady 14-5-61 to 6-4-08' (above) arriving at Flimby on 10th December 2009 with 2Z31, the 14:00 Maryport - Workington. Class 47/4 No.47501 'Craftsman' is on the rear of the four coach train, which will power the return (2T32) working.

(Overleaf)

This atmospheric view shows No.47501 (page 46) on the rear of 2Z33, the 15:10 Maryport - Workington, shortly after leaving Maryport on 10th December 2009 behind No.37423. The eye is automatically drawn towards the steelworks and wind turbines, which overpower the town of Workington, six miles further down the coast.

No.37423 'Spirit of The Lakes', top 'n' tailed with Class 47/7 No.47790 'Galloway Princess' (page 47), heads past Siddick on 1st December 2009, with 2T26, the 11:20 Workington - Maryport.   Fred Kerr (3)

On the last day of November 2009, Class 47/4 No.47832 'Solway Princess' (above) heads past Maryport signalbox and away with 2T24, the 10:30 departure for Workington - No.37423 is at the rear of this four coach formation, comprising one ex-InterCity liveried and three DRS liveried Mk2 coaches. Ian Ball

The following day, 1st December 2009, Class 47/7 No.47790 'Galloway Princess' (below) tails 2T26, the 11:20 Workington - Maryport, as No.37423 'Spirit of The Lakes' leads away from the camera at Siddick. Fred Kerr

Another wind turbine stands tall in a partially flooded field at Siddick, as an almost 'model-like' 2T26, the 11:20 Workington - Maryport, (above) passes by on 10th December 2009. The train is top 'n' tailed by Class 47/4 No.47501 'Craftsman' and No.37610 'TS (Ted) Cassady 14-5-61 to 6-4-08'. Fred Kerr

With plenty of 'clag' and a rapidly setting winter sun, No.47832 (below) accelerates away from the Flimby station stop with the 17th leg of the daily diagram - 2Z33, the 15:10 Maryport - Workington. Ian Ball

DRS provide the power ....

During week-commencing 8th February, NXEA (National Express East Anglia) find themselves short of units at Norwich Crown Point, probably due to a backlog of maintenance following the wintry weather. Consequently, a loco-hauled replacement diagram is instigated, consisting of 9 round trips on the 'Wherry Lines' between Norwich and Great Yarmouth / Lowestoft using DRS Class 47s, No.47712 *'Pride of Carlisle'* and No.47832 *'Solway Princess'*.

The two locos top 'n' tail a consist of two Mk3 vehicles + DVT and, as an added bonus for enthusiasts, DRS Class 20/3 No.20304 deputises for failed No.47832 on 9th February.

The full diagram is:

2P04	0634, Norwich - Great Yarmouth		2P03	0717, Great Yarmouth - Norwich
2J66	0754, Norwich - Lowestoft		2J69	0842, Lowestoft - Norwich
2P10	0936, Norwich - Great Yarmouth		2P11	1017, Great Yarmouth - Norwich
2J72	1057, Norwich - Lowestoft		2J75	1142, Lowestoft - Norwich
2P16	1236, Norwich - Great Yarmouth		2P17	1317, Great Yarmouth - Norwich
2P20	1436, Norwich - Great Yarmouth		2P21	1517, Great Yarmouth - Norwich
2J82	1557, Norwich - Lowestoft		2J85	1647, Lowestoft - Norwich
2P28	1736, Norwich - Great Yarmouth		2P27	1817, Great Yarmouth - Norwich
2P32	1936, Norwich - Great Yarmouth		2P33	2017, Great Yarmouth - Norwich

No.47832 (above) trails 2J72 across the swing bridge at Reedham as No.47712 heads away towards Lowestoft. The red flag shows the bridge is operational; two red flags mean the bridge will not be opened. Historically, the first swing bridge at Reedham opened in 1847 on behalf of the Lowestoft Railway and Harbour Company; modernised in 1904 by the Great Eastern Railway, when the line became double track. The swing bridge rests on two end piers, with a central pivot pier constructed of brick with timber piles, which supports the central pivots when the bridge is closed. Three, 139ft long, wrought iron girders bear the live load and these rotate when the bridge swings to allow passage of river traffic. Two truss girders bear the weight of the bridge when it is open. Three other railway swing bridges survive at Oulton Broad, Somerleyton and Trowse.

On 12th February, No.47712 (opposite) tops 2P10, the 09:36 Norwich - Great Yarmouth, at Acle amid the signs that in the eastern counties, Winter is still with us. No.47832 'Solway Princess' is tailing.   Nick Slocombe (2)

OVERLEAF

Page 52:

20304 *(top) is a rarity indeed .... for this loco-hauled 'vice' unit diagram, the cognoscenti enjoy the sights, sounds and smells of vintage motive power. DRS Class 20/3 loco + DVT + 2 Mk3 coaches + an unidentified Class 47, head away from Great Yarmouth on 9th February with 2P21, the 15:17 service to Norwich. Loco-hauled trains have been introduced in East Anglia during February due to a shortage of DMUs at Norwich but, on 9th February, No.20304 deputises following the failure of one of the booked Class 47 locos.* Stuart Chapman

Three days later, it's back to sulzer power, as No.47832 'Solway Princess' (bottom) gets away from Cantley on 2J75, the 11:42 from Lowestoft, in a plume of exhaust. Beet processing is still in full swing at Cantley, the harvest will be a record in terms of yields, if the Eastern Daily Press is to be believed. No.47712 tails. Nick Slocombe

**Wrexham & Shropshire
Snow, Stock & Diversions**

The New Year heralds plenty of interest for enthusiasts who follow Wrexham, Shropshire & Marlyebone Railway loco-hauled services, with plenty of new photographic opportunities: snow in the Chilterns, engineering work between Leamington and Banbury and diversions via the WCML, 'Hybrid' stock and No.67018 *'Keith Heller'* putting in an appearance.

Above: *About six inches of snow falls the night before, much of it being thrown up by No.67012 'A Shropshire Lad' as it approaches Haddenham & Thame Parkway station at speed on 6th January with 1P13, the 11:27 Wrexham - Marylebone, running 20 minutes late. The 14:45 departure from Haddenham to Stratford-upon-Avon is largely hidden by the snow spray as it heads north, the signal not having yet turned to red.* Geoff Plumb

Diversions : *Weekend engineering on the Chiltern route often results in WSMR services being diverted around the London suburbs. On 7th March, diversions are via the WCML and No.67010 (above) is seen in charge of 1P52, the 11:20 Wrexham - Marylebone, speeding through Cheddington station on the 'Up Fast' line, 10 minutes late.*

No.67010 (below) is seen again, approaching South Ruislip station along the former main line from Paddington with 1P01, 07:23 Wrexham - Marylebone, diverted from its normal route due to engineering works north of Banbury. It is routed from Coventry up the WCML to Wembley, then Acton Canal Wharf Junction, Acton Mainline, West Ealing, Greenford, followed by a reversal at South Ruislip to regain its normal route into Marylebone, which is seen to the left of the loco. The train is formed of a 'hybrid' set of Virgin liveried coaches, WSMR silver RFM and the Chiltern liveried DVT No.82302, running around 15 minutes late at this point on Saturday, 30th January.

67018 'Keith Heller' : *As a temporary replacement for No.67015, WSMR use newly painted No.67018 'Keith Heller' (above) on 1P01, the 05:10 Wrexham - Marylebone, which is seen passing Haddenham & Thame Parkway station at full line speed on a filthy 17th February. No.67018 is named in honour of Keith Heller (Co-Chairman of DB Schenker) at a naming ceremony at the NRM in York on 15th January. The loco is personalised with a large maple leaf, to recognise Mr Heller's Canadian nationality, and painted in Canadian National colours.*

Photo Call : *Tree clearance creates a new photographic opportunity. WSMR No.67014 'Thomas Telford' (above) is leading 1P01, the 05:10 Wrexham - Marylebone on 18th March, as it approaches the short Brill Tunnel with DVT No.82303 on the rear of the train and running on time. The tree clearance at this site opens up the view again and is still in progress, apparently in conjunction with the SSSI in the adjacent Rushbeds Wood. SSSI is the abbreviation for 'Site of Special Scientific Interest'.* Geoff Plumb (4)

37218 *(above) amidst the semaphores at Fouldubs Junction, Grangemouth, couples up to 4A13, Grangemouth - Aberdeen, intermodal and now waits for Class 66/4 No.66428 to back onto the train and depart. The date is 15th January and the '37' has arrived (0A13) light engine from Carlisle and is on its way to Aberdeen for a spell of snow plough duties.* Guy Houston

37087 **'Keighley & Worth Valley Railway'** *(above) is seen on a Stoneblower move on 23rd February passing the site of Sutton Park station, running as 6Z16, Doncaster Marshgate - Ashford. The Sutton Park line is 'freight only' and runs from Ryecroft Junction (Walsall) to join the Birmingham - Derby main line at two separate junctions, Castle Bromwich and Water Orton.* David Weake

1Z16, Inverness - Edinburgh The news of the possibility of an HST being 'dragged' from Inverness to Edinburgh on 3rd January by one of the resident DRS Class 37 'Thunderbirds' is something not to be missed! Unfortunately, the train runs too late in the day for any photograph in the sun, but a record of this rare event is well worth having.

Here, Class 37/5 No.37667 (above) hauls 1Z16, the 13:00 Inverness - Edinburgh, (No.43318 leading / No.43307 rear) in the last of the daylight, dropping down from Druimachdair Summit and passing Dalnacardoch. This is way after the sun had gone at 16:02, by which time 1Z16 is running 70+ minutes late having lost at least 50minutes from Aviemore. The train was formed of the stock and power cars off the 'caped' Inverness - London King's Cross.

Upon arrival at Perth, the Class 37 (below) is 'ripped' from the train and Class 67 No.67025 'Western Star' takes over for the final leg of the journey to Edinburgh. A snow-encrusted No.37667 is seen parked up in Platform 3 while the Class 67 prepares to couple-up to the HST. Guy Houston (2)

37425 'Pride of the Valleys / Balchder y Cymoedd' *(above) is employed North of the Border on 'snowplough' duties but, on 12th February, is allocated to head back to Mossend on 6D84, ex-Aberdeen. No.37425 (above) is seen at Aberdeen Waterloo Quay shunting some internationally registered (Number Range 33. 87. 7797. 002 to 039) ICA Calcium Carbonate bogie tank wagons, which will form 6A80 to Aberdeen station.* Steven Robertson

97301

0Z97,
Barrow Hill - Exeter
(Right)

I don't go much for light engine movements, but I make an exception for the appearance of a Network Rail Class 97/3 working in the South West; pretty rare and worthy of a record 'phot'.

On 15th February, No.97301 accelerates through Taunton running as 0Z97, the 08:00 Barrow Hill – Exeter Riverside, route learner; photographed from 40 Steps, which is an excellent vantage point.

Rob Sherwood

97302

5Z97, Derby - Tyseley
(Centre)

No.97302 is out on 18th May working a 5Z97, Derby RTC - Tyseley LMD, ECS move and is seen on the Birmingham Snow Hill - Tyseley - Leamington Spa main line at Small Heath.

On the skyline is the British Telecom Tower, a well-known landmark and the tallest building in Birmingham at 500 feet. Construction began in July 1963, completed in September 1965, becoming operational in December 1966. David Weake

97303 + 97304
1Z12,
Shrewsbury - Machynlleth
(Right)

On 23rd January, these two Network Rail Class 97/3s have a run out down the Cambrian Line. In this view, Nos.37903 + 37904 are heading along the single line at Abermule, which is in the valley of the River Severn, between Welshpool and Newtown.

The duo are operating in top 'n' tail formation with No.97303 leading the Network Rail test train; 1Z12, Sutton Bridge Jct - Machynlleth. Jamie Squibbs

On the Blocks' .... *Class 37/4 No.37425 'Pride of the Valleys' (above) sits on the blocks at Glasgow Central after arriving with 5M11, Polmadie - Glasgow Central, sleeper stock to form 1M11, the 23:40 sleeper to London Euston, hauled on 10th May by EWS-liveried Class 90 No.90029.* Guy Houston

Looking immaculate after receiving attention at Barrow Hill, No.37409 (below) leads No.37423 and the saloon 'Caroline' at London Waterloo prior to departing as 2Z01 to Southampton on 15th June. This is quite an occasion, as it's the first time a DRS 37/4 visits London Waterloo and it is believed to be the first revenue-earning outing for No.37409, since being reinstated to traffic on 27th May. Michael Wright

'To Russia with Love' ....

37610 'T.S. (Ted) Cassady 14.5.61 to 6.4.08' *(above) has had a little power applied by the driver to keep his train running at 60mph, as it approaches Broomfleet Station on 5th July heading 6Z26, the 08:00 Sellafield - Hull Hedon Road, low level waste train. The ISO boxes contain Uranium, loaded in small 'keg-like' drums, returning to Russia, after reprocessing at the Thorp nuclear plant at Sellafield. Sister loco No.37611 is 'Dead in Tow' on the rear.*

Broomfleet is on the main line linking Selby and Hull and has one of (if not the) longest stretches of continuous straight track on the network. The section between Gilberdyke and Ferriby is also still controlled by semaphore signalling, as we can see in this image. James Skoyles

---

Overleaf:

'Little & Large' ....

37425 'Pride of the Valleys / Balchder y Cymoedd' *(page 62) is sharing the limelight in this excellent image with the fishing boat 'Benbola', which is moored in Bowling Harbour on the River Clyde. When it becomes clear the last operational DBS Class 37 is booked to operate a ballast train onto the Oban line on 27th April, the photograper hastily arranges a day off work. In the first of three views, No.37425 ambles through Bowling with 6K20, Mossend - Dalmally; an image which is quite a contrast to the one below!* Guy Houston

37610 'T.S. (Ted) Cassady 14.5.61 to 6.4.08' *(page 63) provides a superb, detailed, close up look of a Class 37 in action. On 10th December 2009, No.37610 top 'n' tails No.47501 'Craftsman' (out of view) heading south at Flimby on the Cumbrian Coast with 2Z23, the 10:02 Maryport - Workington.* Fred Kerr

37425

In the Wrekin .... *a temporary footbridge is installed at Shifnal station, which provides a different viewpoint of the town. On 22nd April, No.37425 'Pride of the Valleys' (above) runs through with 6W91, the 02:38 Pwllheli - Bescot, ballast empties. Interestingly, the 'Wrekin' is actually a hill, but also an area of East Shropshire around Wellington, Telford and Shifnal.* Mike Hemming

On the same date, the late running train is seen again with No.37425 (below) passing Bonemill Bridge (between Cosford and Shifnal on the Wolverhampton - Shrewsbury main line) with two sets of Autoballasters. Ian Ball

On the West Highland .... No.37425 (above) idles during ballasting in the Pass of Brander, where the line squeezes between the lower slopes of Ben Cruachan and Loch Awe. Of note, are the stone signals in the Pass, controlled by wires along the north side of the line, which will be broken under the weight of boulders or snow, thus changing the signals to 'Danger' and so warn approaching trains to stop. This system dates back to 1882 and there are 16 such signals spaced at intervals of about a quarter of a mile.

Earlier, No.37425 (below) storms up the 1 in 69 gradient to reach Arrochar and Tarbet station with 6K20, Mossend - Dalmally, very reminiscent of former delights on the West Highland Line, weather and all!   Guy Houston (2)

6Z90, Tyne Dock - Sheerness

Working of the Year

Background:

The sight and sound of a Class 37, let alone a pair, working a 'proper' freight is something not to be missed and photographers the length and breadth of the country turn out in force to record this rare event.

The service concerned is a DRS-operated flow of scrap metal on behalf of EMR (European Metals Recycling) from Tyne Dock to Thamesteel steelworks at Sheerness on the Isle of Sheppey. The Company has been intending to use its Class 37s on these services due to the diagram being beyond the fuel range of a low-emission Class 66/4 loco.

The first train runs on 17th April with Class 37/5s Nos.37510 + 37667 entrusted to the diagram; the pair working this service on several occasions.

The consist is formed, quite interestingly, of former Sheerness (Co-Steel) bogie scrap wagons now owned by VTG, numbered in the VTG 3100 - VTG 3159 series, comprising:

3122	3154	3116	3118	3105	3103	3107	3113
3153	3150	3139	3138	3128	3126	3104	3133

In view of the interest generated by this working, a number of images are included at various locations on the route.

> **Barnes** : *Starting off this frenzy of 6Z70 / 6Z90 activity, here in Southern Region territory on 23rd April, the two Class 37/5 locos Nos.37667 + 37510 (top) slowly pass through Barnes station in order to leave the Richmond main line and cross the River Thames via Barnes Bridge with 6Z70, the 08:37 Sheerness - Tyne Dock, scrap empties. DRS appear to be keen to use more 'heritage' traction on 'non-nuclear' traffic and enthusiasts will certainly welcome this!* Michael Wright

Derby : *The two 'tractors' are certainly an impressive sight on a 'real' freight .... Nos.37510 + 37667 (above), both fitted with mini ploughs, roll into Derby station with 6Z90, on 21st April. Fortunately, the sun is shining today, unlike the previous week when the first train ran in dull and overcast conditions.* Michael Wright

Overleaf:

Barow Hill *(Page 68): Earlier, on 21st April, Nos.37510 + 37667 are seen on the 'Old Road' hurrying through the cutting at Barrow Hill heading for Chesterfield with 6Z90, the 08:13 Tyne Dock - Sheerness.* Mick Tindall

Ratcliffe *(Page 69): The cooling towers at Ratcliffe power station loom large and dominate the skyline, as the pair of 37s continue their long journey south along the Midland Main Line.* Lee Marshall

Berkswell : *Following the loaded run on 15th April, the return is scheduled for Saturday, 17th April, routed through the Midlands area via Coventry - Stechford - Aston - Bescot - Sutton Park - Water Orton, thus providing the rare sight of DRS 37s working something other than a short train or one or two nuclear flasks. Nos.37667 + 37510 (below) pass Balsall Common, Berkswell, just west of Coventry, with the empties.* Peter Tandy

Wellingborough : *Nos.37667 + 37510 (above) sweep through the reverse curves at Irthlingborough Road, Wellingborough, on 23rd April with empty JXAs, running as 6Z70, the 10:14 Sheerness - Stockton, on this particular occasion.* Nigel Gibbs

Leicester : *Wednesday, 21st April, proves to be a cracking day for photography with long spells of spring sunshine as is proven with this view of Nos.37510 + 37667 (below) accelerating past Wigston South Junction, Leicester, with 6Z90 loaded scrap. The line diverging to the left leads to Hinckley, the Bardon Aggregates quarry at Croft and, finally, Nuneaton on the West Coast Main Line.* Lee Marshall

Radwell: *Further south on 21st April, the two 37s (above) scurry along the 'Up' slow line at Radwell, south of Sharnbrook Junction at 16:53hrs on 6Z90, the 08:37 Tyne Dock - Sheerness loaded scrap. Of interest, the rear half of the train is crossing the Great Ouse and the train will cross the river seven times in approximately 6 miles between Sharnbrook and Bedford. At this stage, the train is running 15 minutes early, but will stand at Bedford North for some 90-minutes due to a signal failure south of Bedford.* Nigel Gibbs

Chesterfield: *On 11th April, Nos.37667 + 37510 (below) head 6Z70, the 10:08 Sheerness - Tyne Dock, JXA empties north through Chesterfield at Tapton Junction, about to take the 'Old Road' to Barrow Hill.* Lee Marshall

37423 '**Spirit of the Lakes / Pride of the Valleys**' *(above) is running through Birnam Wood, Dunkeld on the Highland Line, which is a beautiful spot for photography, as this image will surely testify. Due to the non-availability of an operative Class 37 loco, DBS hire-in Class 37/4 No.37423 to work 6K12, the 13:05 Mossend - Garve, ballast on 5th July, comprising a 5-vehicle 'Autoballaster' set. Garve is located on the Inverness - Kyle of Lochalsh line and means No.37423 faces a round trip of more than 400 miles to fulfil its ballasting duties.* Jim Ramsay

37688 'Kingmoor TMD' **+ 37229** 'Jonty Jarvis' *(above) turn up on a special working which somehow almost manages to sneak under the radar and runs without too much publicity. On Thursday, 26th November 2009, the DRS 37s run light engine to Gloucester to collect a set of TEA tanks and JNA box wagons, destined for Long Marston, and the novelty of seeing DRS 37s on a decent length train is not to be missed. The train (6Z40, Gloucester - Long Marston) approaches Evesham station where a token exchange will take pace.* Peter Tandy

37607 + 37059 *(below) provide a 'close encounter' and perfect timing. Just as a southbound Virgin 'Pendolino' hurtles past, ensures a good shot of the '37s' slowing for a red signal at Cheddington, whilst hauling 4M71, Tilbury - Daventry, 'Sugarliner' on 2nd June - Well done that man!* Geoff Plumb

37401 *(above) is the only EWS-liveried '37' left in traffic on 25th November 2009 and it is working the Blackburn 'trip' (6N42 / 6F42). On the return 6F42, Blackburn - Arpley, No.37401 passes Balshaw Junction with a consist of three 2-axle MTA open wagons and a number of IWA / IWB 'Cargowaggons'.* Fred Kerr

37608 + 37601 *(below) are deployed on early 'Sandite' duties on 5th July, due to bad railhead conditions in Teesside, working in the usual top 'n' tail formation. DRS Class 37/6 No.37608 leads and spraying gets under way, as the train heads east at South Bank with 6Z41, York - York, which is running via Tees Dock.* Ian Ball

37425 'Pride of the Valleys / Balchder y Cymoedd' *(above) on 30th April has charge of the Arpley 'chemical' trip and is seen at Acton Bridge with 6F62, the 11:12 FO Runcorn - Warrington Arpley, via Northwich. This particular '37' was named 'Concrete Bob' in a previous life.* Jamie Squibbs

37676 'Loch Awe' *(below) is busily 'clagging' away at Ardmore level crossing, south east of Craigendoran, on 6th June with 6Y45, Fort Wiliam - Mossend, 'Alcan' tanks; dull, wet and extremely miserable, but a record all the same. No.66729 'Derby County' had failed and the WCRC '37' came to the rescue.* Alastair Blackwood

37611 + 37059 (above) rekindle fond memories of an occasion back in May 1997, when two Mainline-liveried Class 37s (No.37023 + No.37379) were photographed passing the same spot at Crawford with a heavy 6L80, Deanside - Wisbech, petfood train. On 3rd June, the two DRS 'tractors' pass the same spot making a healthy din building up speed on the ascent of Beattock Bank with 6M82, Coatbridge - Daventry, intermodal.
Alastair Blackwood

37685 (below) along with GWR pannier tank 0-6-0 No.9466 make a rare visit of a loco-hauled train to the Liskeard - Looe branch on 19th September, top 'n' tailing four trips along the scenic Cornish Line. The colourful ensemble is seen passing Sandplace with 2W18, the 17:55 Looe - Liskeard in the last of the day's sunshine.
Jamie Squibbs

37409 'Lord Hinton' **+ 37423** 'Spirit of the Lakes' *(above) pass Craigo in the early evening sun, with 1Z22, Aberdeen - Aberdeen, 'Northern Belle' on Sunday, 5th September, travelling via Fife. The DRS '37s' have been turned out because DBS cannot supply locos for the train!*

37676 'Loch Rannoch' **+ 37516** *(below) look quite stunning in this previoulsy published image, but I make no apology for doing so again. They are passing through beautiful Glen Lochy on Bank Holiday Monday, 3rd May, with a North East Railtour charter, 1Z37, Newcastle - Oban.* Jim Ramsay (2)

37706 (above) is seen behind Southern Railway N15 'King Arthur' Class 4-6-0 steam loco No.30777 'Sir Lamiel' *slowing for a signal stop at Worting Junction with 1Z86, the 08:45 London Victoria - Swanage, 'Swanage Belle'. Due to the hot summer and risk of a lineside fire, Network Rail order a diesel to assist and take most of the strain to prevent the steam loco emitting sparks - No.37706 has the honour!*　　Simon Howard

37423 'Spirit of the Lakes' + 37059 (below) with No.20305 on the rear, pass Eccles Road on 24th April with *Spitfire Railtour's return 1Z40, the 17.18 Norwich - Crewe, 'Broadsman' charter. Class 37s are popular with operators as their good 'Route Availability' means they can go pretty well anywhere.*　　Nigel Gibbs

60040 *'Territorial Army Centenary'* The lights are on and daylight is fading fast at Westerleigh oil terminal. No.60040 (above) waits to marshal the two sections of TEA bogie tanks, which will form 6E41 petroleum empties to Lindsey on 16th January. Despite the reduced number of operational Class 60s running, this flow remains a 'Tug' banker!   Simon Howard

This is Pilmoor, 15-miles north of York on the famous 'racing stretch' on the ECML between York and Darlington. On 1st September, No.60040 (below) passes with 6N45, Scunthorpe - Redcar, empties, formed of SSA 2-axle open scrap wagons.   Ian Ball

'A Sorry Start'

Following mass withdrawals of the Class 60 fleet in 2009, enthusiasts have little grounds for optimism as 2010 and a new decade dawns. In fact, on the first working day of the New Year, Monday, 3rd January, only **5** active 'tugs' are showing on TOPS (see below) and this number remains low until more '60s' are required to satisfy a shortfall of DBS motive power caused by the RHTT season.

Number	Pool	Location	Allocated
60009	WCBI	Lindsey	6N03, Lindsey - Jarrow
60049	WCAK	Peak Forest	6F05, Tunstead - Oakleigh
60059	WCBI	Doncaster	
60071	WCBI	Doncaster	
60096	WCAM	En Route	6F20, Warrington Old Jct - Liverpool BT

A further 4 Class 60s (Nos.60039 / 051 / 063 and 094) are in the WNTR (Tactical Reserve) Pool.

60074 'Teenage Spirit' *Celebrity 'tug' No.60074 'Teenage Spirit' (above) approaches Water Orton on 1st March, with a humble load of 2-axle departmental wagons, running as 6D44, Bescot – Toton. Unless required at Toton TMD for exam, it will probably be seen again passing through this freight 'Hotspot' some five hours later on the return 6G45, Toton - Bescot.* Scott Turner

(Overleaf)

60085 'MINI Pride of Oxford' *(Page 82): A splendid composition .... on Monday, 8th March, No.60085 is seen passing Chinley with 6H03, Oakleigh - Tunstead, limestone empties. The consist is formed of Brunner Mond JEA bogie aggregate hoppers, which are unique to this particular flow. Unfortunately, you cannot help but notice the ugly Pallisade fencing on the left of view which does nothing to enhance the picture, hopefully this will be obscured by lineside vegetation in the future.*

60054 'Charles Babbage' *(Page 83): A 'tug' banker is the Lindsey - Jarrow petroleum flow and the returning empties being high on a photographers shopping list! Here, No.60054 pauses long enough under York's famous trainshed canopy on 27th February for a perfect exposure to be gained of 6D77, Jarrow - Lindsey, petroleum empties. York station is situated on a loop line turning fully 150° and, during electrification of the ECML, the overhead catenary was constructed as unobtrusively as possible to preserve the aesthetics!* Lee Marshall (2)

60071 *'Ribblehead Viaduct'* on 6E41

The daily oil train from Lindsey refinery to Westerleigh, and return empties, continues to produce a Class 60 on most occasions. Although the light isn't really right to photograph 6E41 at this time of day, a record of it's passing is worthwhile in this rather misty and backlit, yet attractive, part of Worcestershire. No.60071 (above) is seen heading north near Abbotswood Junction on 16th March with the long train of empty tanks. Peter Tandy

This is a particular shot the photographer has been wanting for a long time and he achieves his goal on 5th March. No.60071 (below) heads for Lindsey oil refinery with 6E41 Westerleigh - Lindsey, empty oil tanks, against a marvellous sunset and amidst some of Barnetby's finest semaphores. James Skoyles

60096 on *'Furnace Burden'*

A real treat on a Saturday .... one of the remaining members of the Class 60 fleet in action in the North East of England. On 13th March, No.60096 (above) has charge of 6Z03, ex-Santon, and is en-route to Redcar with a rake of empty tipplers to be loaded with 'Furnace Burden'. The train is passing South Bank, Teesside. **Ian Ball**

Having collected its payload from Redcar, No.60096 (below) is seen again passing Church Fenton with 6A03, the 11:34 (SO) Redcar - Santon, and according to the photographer, this so called 'Furnace Burden, seems rather like Pulverised Flyash, given the way it was blowing off the tipplers. 6A03 is routed via Sherburn in Elmet - Hambleton West Junction - Temple Hirst Junction - Joan Croft Junction - Applehurst Junction. Nick Slocombe

60040 *'The Territorial Army Centenary'* Just minutes before sunset on Saturday, 30th January, No.60040 (above) passes Oakley, near Bedford, with a rake of bogie tanks (TDAs and TEAs) forming 6E38, the 13:05 Colnbrook - Lindsey, rare '60' haulage these days! Nigel Gibbs

60074 *'Teenage Spirit'* Back on old stamping grounds. Working Iron Ore 'trips' between Immingham and Scunthorpe steelworks on 11th August, No.60074 (below) heads 6K22, the 09:35 Santon - Immingham, empty Iron Ore tipplers, past the popular 'photospot' of New Barnetby. Mick Tindall

60051 *"Never going to be a classic, but the sun manages to make a slight shadow"* as No.60051 (above) passes Edington on the Berks & Hants, 17th March, heading 6M20, Whatley - St Pancras, formed of Hanson-liveried JHA Bogie Hoppers. A rare sight, but a '60' back on the Mendip circuit! Kevin Poole

60096 *"Back where they belong"....* No.60096 (below) powers 6B13, Robeston - Westerleigh, loaded petroleum tanks past Llandeilo Junction, as dawn is breaking a little over 7am on 15th April. The last time a '60' turned up on this working was four months ago on 12th December 2009. Mark Thomas

60074 (above) is seen on what was once a solid Class 60 turn on the Great Western Main Line, the Robeston to Theale tanks. On Tuesday, 20th April, the diagram 'drops' a '60' and No. '074 is seen heading 6B33, Theale - Robeston, along the embankment at South Marston, on the outskirts of Swindon.
Martin Buck

60096 (below) finds itself on 21st April, allocated to work 6K05, the 12:21 Carlisle Yard - Crewe Basford Hall, departmental service of concrete sleepers, which is seen passing Ais Gill Viaduct on the Settle & Carlisle; I don't know how often a '60' produces on this turn, but it must be a very rare occurrence.
Donald Cameron

The Rape of Elford In late spring, fields come alive with oil-seed rape, providing an almost luminous glow of blinding yellow - love it or hate it, it certainly brightens things up!

On 17th May, No.60049 (above) heads south several hours late after a brief pause in Elford loop for pathing purposes with loaded EWS-branded TEAs, running as 6V98, Lindsey - Westerleigh, Loaded Tanks. Earlier in the day and travelling in the opposite direction, this broadside view shows No.60071 'Ribblehead Viaduct' (below) heading north with the return leg of 6V98 - 6E41, Westerleigh - Lindsey, empty petroleum tanks. This popular spot is 4 miles north of Tamworth on the Birmingham - Derby line. David Weake (2)

60049 *November 2009, Freightliner loses the Humber - Kingsbury petroleum contract to DBS, which means one of their locos will haul the distinctive blue-livery TEA petroleum tanks for the first time. On 13th May, a Class 60 has the honour and No.60049 (above) heads through Lincoln Central with 6E54, Kingsbury - Humber Oil Refinery, and a full load of 30 TEA tanks - an impressive sight!*   James Skoyles

On the previous day, No.60049 (below) heads out of Derby with 6M18, Doncaster Decoy - Toton, departmental service formed of engineers wagons, including two YKA 'Osprey' Borail wagons, fitted with yellow stanchions to enable 30ft and 60ft track panels to be secured without the need of strapping.   David Weake

60013 *'Robert Boyle'*

Wednesday, 7th July. This is a 'grey' day, both in terms of the weather and the return to traffic of grey-liveried No.60013 'Robert Boyle'. The loco arrives in South Wales on 6V19, Rotherham - Margam, steel and is immediately allocated to 0A11, Margam - Robeston / 6A11, Robeston - Theale. No.60013 (opposite) is seen exiting Lonlas Tunnel on the Swansea District line heading for Robeston and then, 24-hours later, the loco (above) is seen again having arrived back at Margam Knuckle yard with 6B33, Theale - Robeston, 'Murco' empties.

On 28th July, the same day as No.59206 works the Margam - Trostre 'trips', an added bonus is the allocation of No.60013 to 6B07, Margam - Robeston. On the Swansea District Line, No.60013 (below) passes the site of the junction serving the now demolished Llandarcy refinery and boarded up signal box.　　　　Mark Thomas (3)

60011 Now, a rare appearance, is a 'Tug' on 6E38, the 13:54 Colnbrook - Lindsey. Ex-Mainline liveried No.60011 (above) passes the former railway cottages at Oakley (near Bedford) on the Midland 'Down Slow' line on 15th July; see Page 86 for another view of a '60' working 6E38.   Nigel Gibbs

60040 'The Territorial Army Centenary' A scene from the East Coast Main Line in mid-April, depicting No.60040 (below) working a solid 'tug' turn - the 'Jarrow Tanks' - passing Black Banks, Darlington, with 6D43, Jarrow - Lindsey. As is the case with most Lindsey petroleum trains, it is the returning empties which provide the best photographic opportunities for this particular flow.   Ian Ball

60039 *Storm clouds gather as No.60039 (above) approaches Chepstow on 11th June with 6B47, Westerleigh - Robeston, empty petroleum tanks. This, and the loaded train (6B13), is routed via Severn Tunnel, Chepstow, Gloucester, Standish Jct and Yate in order to gain access to the oil terminal at Westerleigh.*

60074 'Teenage Spirit' *On 23rd April, the loaded 6B13, Robeston - Westerleigh, petroleum tanks forms the centrepiece with No.60074 (below) heading south at Wickwar, about 3 miles away from Yate, the point where No.60074 will leave the Bristol - Birmingham main line and proceed on the single line track to the oil terminal. Enhancing the view is the the blackthorn blossom, in full bloom.* Dave Gower (2)

60051 *As is so often the plight of a railway photographer, the weather does not play ball just when you would like! In absolute monsoon conditions, No.60051 (above) passes Ponthir (near Caerleon, Newport) on 2nd April with 6M86, Llanwern - Dee Marsh, loaded steel.* Jamie Squibbs

60059 *'Swinden Dalesman'* *Anything will do! The lack of suitable traction at Mossend means a surprise trip for Loadhaul Class 60, No.60059 'Swinden Dalesman' on 15th September. After running light to Polmadie (0M11), No.60059 (below) then works 5M11, Polmadie - Glasgow Central, ECS for the 1M11 'Beds' to London Euston and is seen 'on the blocks' upon arrival at Central station.* Guy Houston

60073 'Cairn Gorm' On 3rd September, DBS two-tone Grey Class 60, No.60073 'Cairn Gorm' *(above) passes the Brickworks, approaching Ramsey Road Level Crossing, near Whittlesea. The '60' is leading 6L39, Mountsorrel - Trowse, which consists entirely of ex-RMC 'JGAs'.* James Welham

60096 *A new addition to the working timetable in 2010 is 6X01, the 09:41 (TThO) Scunthorpe - Eastleigh, conveying new lengths of continuous welded rail. It is a 'Q', which means it can turn up on any day of the week and, on 23rd April, it is seen passing Hatton North Junction, hauled by No.60096 (below) running a few minutes early. After working 6X16, No.60096 returns light engine from Eastleigh to Scunthorpe.* Peter Tandy

60091 *This is the line that takes freight trains from the Leeds - Doncaster Mainline over the EMCL near Joan Croft Junction and onto the 'Freight Only' Joan Croft - Applehurst - Stainforth line. No.60091 (above) is seen here passing Tilts Lane with TEA tanks in tow that form 6E32, the 08:55 Preston Docks - Lindsey, empty Bitumen tanks; the days of these TEAs are numbered and are soon to replaced by a new build.* **James Skoyles**

60071 '*Ribblehead Viaduct*' *Battledown is the junction to the west of Basingstoke where the lines to Eastleigh and Andover diverge. On 21st September, No.60071 (below) passes with loaded Network Rail 'Falcon' Bogie Ballast Wagons, forming 6O26, Hinksey - Eastleigh, departmental.* **Simon Howard**

60074 'Teenage Spirit' *Within a three day period, No.60074 ends up working two very contrasting trains and not a petroleum train in sight! On 30th September, having found its way to Westbury from Eastleigh, No.60074 (above) approaches Crofton on the 'Berks & Hants' in some weak sunshine, heading a rake of loaded ex-RMC JGA stone hoppers, which form 6M20, Whatley - St.Pancras.* Steven King

Meanwhile, three days earlier on 27th September, No.60074 (below) is a very surprising choice of loco to take some empty coaching stock back to Eastleigh from Toton. The train (5Z78) is seen here approaching Mill Hill Broadway, running adjacent to the M1 Motorway and, approximately, 80 minutes late. Alan Hazelden

Left: *The sun refuses to shine to mark the arrival of the first Class 70 in the English capital.*

On 3rd December 2009, No.70001 is approaching Caledonian Road and Barnsbury on the North London Line with a well-loaded 4L93, Lawley Street - Felixstowe, freightliner.

No.70001 will become a regular on this daily diagram (4L93 / 4M93) which links the West Midlands and Britain's busiest deep-sea container port. Alan Hazelden

Background : On 26th November 2007, Freightliner UK and General Electric announce 'Project Genesis' involving the design of a new type of freight loco to fit British loading gauge, named 'PowerHaul'. The new loco matches older types in terms of haulage capacity but is more fuel efficient. The first model carries GE designation PH37ACmi and Freightliner placed an initial order for 30 locos (Nos.700001 - 70030), designated Class 70 under TOPS although, originally, it was expected they would receive a TOPS classification of Class 68.

Specification : The Class 70 utilizes a GE PowerHaul P616 diesel engine rated at 3,690 hp, constructed at GE's engine manufacturing plant in Grove City, Pennsylvania, United States. The loco also meets European emission regulations. It is similar in appearance to a Class 58 with a hood unit design, narrow body and the cabs accessed from the rear via exterior walkways on the narrow part of the hood. The distinctive front end shape is due to crashworthiness features and the cab is fitted with air conditioning and acoustic insulation.

In Service : Nos.70001 and 70002, arrive in Britain on 8th November 2009 at Newport Docks and No.70001 is named *'Powerhaul'* at Leeds on 24th November 2009, followed by its maiden run on 11th December 2009 hauling a Felixstowe freightliner.

Nos.70004 - 70006 soon follow, although Nos.70007 - 70012 are not scheduled to arrive in the UK until late autumn. Initial duties are confined to freightliners (Felixstowe - Lawley Street) and power station Coal flows (Avonmouth - Rugeley / Ellesmere Port - Fiddlers Ferry).

A snapshot of the Class 70 fleet on the morning of 6th April is:

Loco	*Pool*	*Location*	*Allocation*
70001	DFGI	Ipswich	4M93, Felixstowe - Lawley Street
70002	DFGH	Crewe, Basford Hall	
70003	DFGH	Stoke Gifford	
70004	DFGH	Garston	6F02, Ellesmere Port - Fiddlers Ferry
70005	DFGH	Leeds, Midland Road	
70006	DFGH	Leeds, Midland Road	

70002

This is a perfect study of a Class 70 loco, dubbed 'Ugly' by some enthusiasts. This is, perhaps, a little unfair, as these locos, in my opinion, are a breath of fresh air and will surely become more popular as time goes by! No.70002 (opposite) is seen in full sun at Stoke Gifford yard, Bristol, on 11th February. Steven King

Rugeley Coal

70004 *(top left) passes Hednesford signalbox on 28th June with 4V61, the 16:55 Rugeley - Stoke Gifford, HHA empties, and enters the site of the original London & North Western Railway station, which closed to passengers and goods traffic in January and September 1965, respectively.*

Much of the seven miles between Ryecroft Junction (Walsall) and Rugeley is still being signalled by semaphore and there are three signalboxes on the line at Bloxwich, Hednesford and Rugeley Town.

70006 *(above) is seen on a wet and dull 12th March at Tame Bridge Parkway, one-mile south east of Bescot, with loaded HHAs, running as 6Z70, Avonmouth - Rugeley; the train reporting number ('70') being quite appropriate bearing in mind the Class of loco hauling the train!*

As a trial, the train is routed through the West Midlands area via:

Stourbridge Junction - Rowley Regis - Soho East Junction - Perry Barr North Junction - Bescot.

However, the gradient of the line around Old Hill Tunnel proves too much for the Class 70 and subsequent coal flows are re-routed via Severn Tunnel, Hereford and Cosford. David Weake (2)

Fiddlers Ferry Coal

70006 (above) is seen on 6F02, the 12:07 Ellesmere Port - Fiddlers Ferry, loaded HHA / HXAs on 3rd March heading along the 'Down Arpley Branch' towards Arpley and then Latchford Sidings for a reversal; this flow is the first Fiddlers Ferry diagram to attract Class 70 traction. The vantage point is Slutchers Lane roadbridge, which overlooks Arpley Yard where a variety of wagons can be seen, including a pristine CTA Bogie Brine Tank Wagon.

70004 (below) approaches Helsby station on 2nd August with 4F03, the 15:15 Fiddlers Ferry - Ellesmere Port, empty HHAs. The peg is 'off', which indicates that No.70004 is about to leave the Warrington - Chester main line and take the Hooton line in order to reach its destination. Fred Kerr (2)

70003 'On Tour'

On Saturday, 17th April, No.70003 becomes the first member of the Class to be summoned for railtour duties, allocated to 1Z66, the 04:54 Swindon - Leeds, the 'Yorkshire Dalesman'; the '70' working the Crewe - Carnforth - Hellifield - Leeds - Hatfield & Stainforth (and return) section. No.70003 + No.66154 (DIT) (above) approach Settle Junction off the 'Little North Western Line' from Carnforth. **Jamie Squibbs**

Journey's end on the outward leg of the Yorkshire Dalesman' - Hatfield & Stainforth - and having carried out the necessary run-round moves, No.70003 + No.66154 (below) head off back to Leeds. The background is dominated by Hatfield Mine, which started life in 1911 when the first sods were cut to sink the mine shafts, coal production commencing in the Barnsley / Dunsil seam in 1921. **Ian Ball**

Some 80 minutes after passing Settle Junction, the ensemble (above) is seen heading east from Leeds in a cutting between Garforth and Micklefield, viewed from the A656 road bridge. The train is running as 1Z69, the 12:01 Leeds - Leeds, which will cover some 70 miles or so, on its run from Leeds to Hatfield & Stainforth and back.

As a solitary sheep grazes in the field, No.70003 + No.66154 (DIT) (below) pass through the picturesque Yorkshire Dales and the village of Long Preston on the journey home, running as 1Z70, the 15:48 Leeds - Swindon, in what can only be described as lovely Spring evening light. Richard Armstrong (2)

4M93

Since being introduced, No.70001 has found a *'home from home'* working a daily freightliner between Birmingham and Felixstowe:

> 4M93, 14:13 Felixstowe - Lawley Street
> 4L69, 01:12 Lawley Street - Felixstowe

On 9th April, No.70001 (above) passes two On Track Plant machines stabled in the engineers sidings at Junction Road Junction (between Upper Holloway and Gospel Oak on the 'GOBLIN'), while in charge of 4M93, Felixstowe - Lawley Street, freightliner. The loco is traversing the non-electrified Tottenham and Hampstead Line, coasting and making no noise at this point, and will now take the Gospel Oak spur.

The North London Line re-opens for business in early June and a new photo angle is possible at Caledonian Road and Barnsbury, which is now an island platform. On 4th June, slightly later than the image shown below, No.70001 (opposite) emerges from the gloom into glorious sunshine with 4M93. Unfortunately, it does not get much further due to OHLE problems at Camden Road.   Nick Slocombe (2)

Also, earlier on 4th June, No.70001 (below) passes through Stratford station with 4M93.   Richard A. Jones

Down The Lickey

70003 *(above) is seen at Stoke Pound with a rake of empty HYA hoppers on 17th March having descended the Lickey Incline with 4Z70, the 08:53 Rugeley - Stoke Gifford, coal empties. In the distance, 'Lickey Banker' No.66058 (WBLI Pool) can be seen in the distance awaiting its next turn of duty.* Ian Ball

Mountsorrel Ballast

70003 *(below) has a rare excursion away from coal duties on 4th June, unusually deployed on 6U77, the 13:48 (FO) Mountsorrel - Crewe Virtual Quarry, loaded ballast, normally a Class 66/6 turn. The train is passing Wychnor Junction on the Derby - Birmingham main line, formed of IOA 'Gondolas', which carry a UIC code ('Ealnos', in this case) which provides a lot more information pertaining to the vehicle's specification.* David Weake

On the Felixstowe Branch

70001 *(above) is a couple of hundred yards west of Morston Hall LC on the Felixstowe branch, near Trimley. The loco was last seen the previous evening (see Page 106) at Caledonian Road and Barnsbury and is now returning to Birmingham, running as 4L69, Lawley Street - Felixstowe.*
Nick Slocombe

1st Anglo-Scottish 'liner

70001 *(below) is well away from its normal duties (4M93, Felixstowe - Lawley Street & 4L69 return) on 17th August working 4M74, the 14:01 Coatbridge - Crewe Basford Hall, freightliner, normally a solid turn for a pair of Class 86/6s! The train is passing Euxton on the WCML and is the first time a Class 70 works a southbound Anglo-Scottish freightliner.*
Fred Kerr

70005
First '70'
North of the Border

On 16th April, No.70005 becomes the first '70' to venture north of the Border, running light engine (0Z70) from Doncaster to Mossend. No.70005 (above) is seen passing Kirknewton on the Edinburgh - Carstairs line. Guy Houston

.... and here is the first revenue earning service in Scotland.

After working in on 6G05, the 08:28 Ravenstruther - Longannet, on 20th April, No.70005 (below) is seen returning to Mossend with 4C07, the 13:26hrs ex-Longannet, ambling along the Stirling - Alloa - Kincardine line on the north banks of the Firth of Forth with 19 empty HXA bogie hoppers in tow. Alastair Blackwood

Anglo - Scottish Coal

April, sees the start of Class 70s on *FHH* Anglo-Scottish coal flows and the first reported working occurs overnight during 26th / 27th April, when No.70004 works north via the ECML, Tyne Valley and 'GSWR' with empty HYAs, running as 4S95, York Holgate - Killoch.

The empties form 6M32, the 09:55 Killoch - Ratcliffe, loaded service, running via the Settle & Carlisle. With 15 miles of 1 in 100 gradient from Ormside to Ais Gill and 2,000 tonnes on the drawbar, this will test the hauling capabilities of the Class 70 to the full. Initially, Class 70 failures on Anglo-Scottish services become a far too frequent occurrence, but reliability seems to improve during May and June. In fact, there are many initial teething problems with the Class in general.

Here is a snapshot of typical Class 70 loaded services during May / June:

6Z63, 01:43 Chalmerston - Rugeley
6M32, 09:50 Killoch - Fiddlers Ferry
6Z85, 11:00 Ravenstruther - York Holgate
6E72, 20:20 Ravenstruther - Drax

70004 *(above) is seen DIT behind Class 66/5 No.66510, having failed on 6M32 the 09:50 Killoch - Fiddlers Ferry. The train is photographed approaching Kirkconnel on Monday, 17th May, running more than 2 hours late, in an area of the Nith Valley rich in coal. In fact, the opencast mine, which can be seen in the background is called Glenmuckloch, where a conveyor takes the coal 12.2 km to the loading point adjacent to New Cumnock station, officially known as Crowbandsgate.* Donald Cameron

Overleaf:

70006 *(Page 112) is seen on the ex-Glasgow & South Western Railway line six miles east of Sanquhar crossing Enterkine Viaduct on 27th August with an early running 6M27, the 14:30 Killoch - Fiddlers Ferry.* Max Fowler

70006 + 70005 *(Page 113) pass Brock (between Lancaster and Preston) with 6Z63, the 01:43 ex-Chalmerston, on 21st May running to Fiddlers Ferry instead of Ratcliffe power station on this particular day. For the photographer's first sighting of an 'Ugly Betty', what could be better than two for the price of one, albeit only the leading loco providing power.* Neil Harvey

LOCOMOTIVE GALLERY

Anglian 'Choppers'

20305 *(above) is working solo, passing Reedham Junction in hazy sunshine on 24th April with 1Z20, the 11:42 Norwich - Great Yarmouth leg of Spitfire Railtour's 'Broadsman' charter. The tour also features two DRS 37s, No.37059 & No.37423, but a single Class 20 out on the main line is a pleasing sight, as for many months, most of the fleet are out of service 'in store' at Carnforth and Eastleigh.* Nigel Gibbs

20304 + 20301 *(below) are seen heading a short rake of National Express East Anglia Mk3 vehicles through Shenfield on the Great Eastern Main Line on 4th January, running as 5V91, Norwich Crown Point - Ilford. This ECS move is certainly a rare outing for the DRS '20s' compared to their usual flask duties.* Stuart Chapman

20301 + 20304 *(top right) wait to leave Berkeley on 17th March with a FNA wagon, containing a solitary flask, which will form 6M56, Berkeley - Crewe.*
The leading loco is No.20301, named 'Max Joule 1958 - 1999'.

Jamie Squibbs

Two weeks earlier, 3rd March, the pair are seen again but, this time, Nos.'301 + '304 (below) are seen on the branch with the inward service, 6V73 ex-Crewe.

The pair will go to Sharpness to run round and then retrace their steps to Berkeley, where the '20's will propel the single FNA into the terminal.

Richard Giles

Severnside Survivor

The Gloucestershire, Sharpness Branch is something of a freight backwater but, after a quiet 2009, has a sort of revival in 2010 with Network Rail undertaking track and replacement sleeper work, plus the Crewe - Berkeley (6V73) nuclear flask trip also restarts.

Furthermore, 2010 marks the 50th Anniversary of this line once being a through route to the Forest of Dean via Britain's 3rd longest rail bridge over the River Severn, tragically part demolished by an oil barge heading for Sharpness Docks on 25th October 1960. The bridge was judged to be beyond economic repair and the Sharpness Line once again became a branch; passenger services lasting only four more years, being withdrawn altogether in November 1964. Consequently, the stations at Sharpness and Berkeley closed.

'S' Stock Moves

20189 + 20142 *(above) in Brunswick Green and BR Blue, respectively, are pictured passing Melton Mowbray signal box on 5th May with 8X09, Old Dalby - Amersham, delivering new 'S' stock to London Underground. Nos.20901 + 20905 are on the rear of the train and all four locos are allocated to the MOLO Pool.*   David Weake

20905 + 20901 *(below) are seen later the same day under the cover of darkness having arrived at Princes Risborough station. The locos are still on the rear at this point but, after a reversal, will lead 8X09 to Aylesbury, where another reversal will take place before 8X09 can resume its journey south.*   Geoff Plumb

20905 + 20901 *(above) are paired with Nos.20189 + 20142 again on 14th May, this time running as 8X23, Derby RTC - Old Dalby, taking a new 'S' set for trials. The train is seen on the little used Coalville line passing Swains Park Sidings, approaching Moira West signal box (out of view).* Guy Houston

20304 + 20305 *(above) are allocated to a new 'GBEE' Loco Pool (created in July) for DRS Class 20/3s on hire to GBRf, along with Nos.20301 / 302 and 308, which have been reinstated. De-branded Nos.20304 + 20305 with another pair (Nos.20301 + 20302 DOR) are seen amidst the angustifolium epilobium, commonly known as Rosebay Willowherb, accelerating down Hatton Bank with 8X09, Old Dalby - Amersham, on 14th July. For the record, 'S' Stock is a class of 'sub-surface' train, being constructed by Bombardier for London Underground, replacing 177 existing trains on the Circle, District, Hammersmith & City and Metropolitan lines, with a new fleet of standardised cars, totalling 191 trains or 1,395 cars.* Peter Tandy

31601 These three images depict Class 31/6 No.31601, which is adorned with Devon & Cornwall branding and painted in British American Railway Services green livery. British American Railway Services was formed to acquire the assets of ECT Rail Holdings in 2008 and some subsidiaries of British American include RMS Locotec, Weardale Railway, Dartmoor Railway, and Devon and Cornwall Railway.

On 4th June, a colourful assortment of rolling stock greets the eye as No.31601 (above) passes through Norwood Junction with 1Z14, the 10:08 Selhurst - Dollands Moor; No.31602 brings up the rear. The train has passed EMU No.377 521 in First Group 'Urban Lights' livery of varying blue with pink, white and blue markings. In the sidings, three EMUs are stabled: Nos.455 811, 377 402 and 377 460, all sporting Southern livery of white & dark green with light green semi-circles at one end, plus a light grey band at solebar level. Richard A. Jones

With the Network Rail DMU based track assessment train being out of service, the current South West diagram is being covered by No.31106 in rail blue, track coach No.999508 and No.31601 in Dartmoor & Cornwall Railway green, albeit without British American vinyls on the bodyside. In this unusual view, No.31601 (opposite) leads the return working from Portbury and passes Ashton on 10th December 2009; part of the structure, which is Brunel's splendid Clifton suspension bridge can be seen on the skyline. Chris Perkins

A delightful composition! On 12th December 2009, No.31601 (below) and No.31106 top 'n' tail 5Z08, the 12:45 Exeter St Davids – Plymouth, skirting the banks of the River Teign at Bishopsteignton. Robert Sherwood

2Q08, Doncaster West Yard - Thornaby

An enjoyable couple of days are spent recording the movements of 2Q08 traversing a selection of interesting lines in West Yorkshire, as the 'Goyles' take a circuitous route to get from Doncaster to Teesside. On 2nd March, Class 31/4 No.31459 'Cerberus' (above) and Class 31/6 No.31602 'Driver Cave Green' top 'n' tail 2Q08 on the climb out of Wakefield towards Oakenshaw Lane with the Horbury Junction to Drax leg of the day's proceedings.

On the following day, No.31602 (above) leads No.31459 out of Bradford Interchange with the Interchange to Forster Square (via Leeds) leg of 2Q08, the 07:33 Doncaster West Yard - Thornaby.

This is a rarely photographed location, due in no small part to the lack of loco-hauled trains in this part of the world. No.31459 (above) trails 2Q08 at Mill Lane Junction as No.31602 heads for Bradford Forster Square. The lines to the left lead to Leeds, the ones towards the bridge go to Halifax.

Finally, a close up view of No.31602 (below) with which to finish, working the Hessle Road - Horbury Junction leg of the journey on 3rd March; 2Q08, the 06:18 ex-Doncaster is approaching Crofton East Junction. Neil Harvey

33207 *'Jim Martin'* (above) is the only narrow bodied 'Slim Jim' Class 33/2 loco operational for main line running. On 9th July, it is passes Dowley Gap, Bingley, in the Aire Valley, in charge of 5Z20, 10:00 Carnforth - York Holgate, ECS. A total of 12 Class 33/2s were built, all to a Loading Gauge of the Tonbridge - Battle line.   Neil Harvey

43052 (above) is bringing up the rear of an East Midlands Trains HST train set, which is an extremely rare visitor to the North East of Scotland, currently on loan to East Coast while their MK4 stock is being refurbished. The front power car (No.43044) is in MML livery and leading 1S03, the 07:10 Leeds - Aberdeen, on 31st August, about to enter Golf Street station, Carnoustie.   Jim Ramsay

47739 *'Robin of Templecombe'* (above), one of three Colas Rail '47s', is taking some TDA & TEA petroleum bogie tanks on 29th March from Bescot to Long Marston for storage. The train (6Z47) is crossing the River Avon at Evesham, running pretty much to time; six TDA bogie tanks are clearly visible. Jamie Squibbs

43468 (above) is Grand Central's recently refurbished MTU powered HST power car (formerly No.43068) and is sporting the Class 180 style livery. On 21st September, it is seen passing Tempsford on the ECML with 1A60, the 06:41 Sunderland - King's Cross; No.43123 is on the rear and, unfortunately, only the leading power is currently carrying the new style livery. Nigel Gibbs

47773 *On 5th December 2009, No.47773 (above), also running as D1755, forms a colourful double act with BR Blue Large Logo No.47580 'County of Essex', taking visitors to Rochester for a 'Dickensian' festival. Train 1Z36, ex-Birmingham Snow Hill, is passing Milton Range, a mile or so from Hoo Junction.* Alan Hazelden

To celebrate the centenary of the Bicester 'Cut-Off' line (Ashendon Junction to Aynho Junction), opened on 1st July 1910, Chiltern Railways run a steam special over the line from Banbury to Princes Risborough. No.D1755 (below), together with GWR 5700 Class 0-6-0 panier tank No.9600, head 5Z28, the 07:00 ECS ex-Tyseley, to form 1Z28, the 10:05 Banbury - Chinnor, 'Centenary Express', hauled by No.9600 on its own. The train is seen at Claydon Crossing at 08:42hrs on Saturday, 3rd July, with seven coaches in tow. Geoff Plumb

47270 'Swift' On 5th June, Class 47/0 No.47270 (right) returns to main line action and works two legs of the 'Fylde Coast Express'.

Five weeks later, on Saturday, 10th July, No.47270 is out again, this time sharing duties with WCRC Class 57 No.57601 on the 'Snowdonia Statesman' charter to Bleanau Ffestiniog. The following day, No.47270 is seen running into Platform 3 at Swindon station with the return ECS (5Z29) to Crewe.

This particular '47' was delivered to Haymarket TMD as No.1971 in October 1965 and under TOPS became No.47270 in March 1974. Steven King

47580 'County of Essex' A convoy of 'heritage' locos returning from the Mid-Norfolk Railway cross 20 Foot River at Turves, between March and Whittlesea, on 23rd March. Class 47/4 No.47580 (above) is towing Nos. 26007, 45133 and 46045, running as 0Z47, the 10:10 Wymondham - Tyseley, via Barrow Hill and the Midland Railway Centre. Nigel Gibbs

(OVERLEAF)

Page 126: No.47580 and No.47826 are a regular pairing in August and, on the 12th, are allocated to work 1Z39, Statesman Rail's 'Sussex Coast Statesman' from Chesterfield to Eastbourne. On the outward journey, No.47580 passes Crawley and the driver applies the power now that the 10:32hrs ex-Victoria EMU has cleared Three Bridges. FHH No.66608 waits to reverse onto the main line with 6Z18, MJA empties to Bardon Hill.

No.47580 is owned by the Stratford 47 Group, currently operated by West Coast Railways, and the loco maintains Stratford TMD's unique touches - grey roof, red buffer beam and cockney sparrow depot symbol. Nick Slocombe

Page 127: 1Z59 has arrived back at Chesterfield, home of the church with a crooked spire, with No.47826 unfortunately leading and No.47580 at the rear. The image is taken at the 'Midnight Hour' using a big 400mm lens from a footbridge 1/4-mile away. Mick Tindall

Boston Steel Colas Rail Class 47s, No.47727 'Rebecca' + No.47749 'Demelza' (above) are pictured on 25th August passing the Lincolnshire village of Heckington on the line from Sleaford to Skegness, approaching Great Hale Drove Number 1 AHB crossing. The service is 6Z56, the 06:15 Washwood Heath - Boston Docks, consisting of 20 empty covered steel wagons. To the left of the picture is the 8-sailed Pocklington Windmill and to the right is the 14th century St Andrew's Church. James Welham

Two ex-BR shunting locos are in use at the Port of Boston, Class 03 No.03112 (D2112) and Class 08 No.08704, the former being illustrated here. On 13th August, No.D2112 (below) crosses over the swing bridge and enters the docks to make a start on bringing the loaded IHA steel carriers to the exchange sidings. Simon Howard

Having entered the dock complex, the shunting loco now takes the IHAs, now loaded with steel, to the exchange sidings, 5-wagons at a time. On 13th August, No.D2112 (above) prepares to take the last 5 wagons from the docks to complete the formation of 6Z57, the 16:51 departure to Washwood Heath. The photographer is fortunate to be invited to view No.D2112 shunting in the docks by the driver / owner of the locos as this is normally a private site with no public access. Despite the poor weather, this proves to be a worthwhile excursion to the Lincolnshire port.

Now that the IHAs have all been loaded, No.66845 (below) waits to leave Boston with 6Z57; a service which commenced in Autumn 2009 and now runs weekly, usually on a Wednesday or Friday. Simon Howard (2)

56312 'Artemis' + 56311 (above) continue to share the work on the 'Boston Steel' flow along with Colas '47s' and '66/8s'. On 26th April, the 'Grids' are turned out to work the outward 6Z56 run to Boston Docks and are seen approaching Nottingham station, photographed from Queen's Bridge.   David Weake

56311 + 56312 'Artemis' (above) are the main interest on 16th April removing a rake of 20 TEA bogie tanks from Long Marston to Bescot. This train (also coded 6Z56!) is seen on the outskirts of Evesham in a cutting, where the sides were cleared in 2009 as part of the first stage of the North Cotswold Line enhancement project. It is a shame there is no 'real' freight along this line but, maybe, when the double track eventually arrives, there will the opportunity for diversions to use it, if the Oxford to Leamington Spa corridor is under possession.   Peter Tandy

56312 *'Artemis'* (above) and a *bizarre tale ....* on 24th May, No.56312 is hired to work 4Z47, Washwood Heath - Tonbridge, taking some container flats to the postal sidings there, only to find the train is too long to fit in the sidings. 4Z47 carries on to Paddock Wood where, after consultations with the powers that be, moves on to Hoo. The train is seen here at New Hythe station with the back drop of the local paper mills.   Alan Hazelden

56100 (above) in the striking Loadhaul colours, albeit faded and weather-beaten, is on its way to European Metals Recycling (EMR) at Kingsbury for scrap. The loco is seen on a low-loader on the M4 Motorway near Bristol on 22nd July and is the last Class 56 to leave South Wales, having been stored at Margam. If the low-loader was classified the same as a steam loco, the wheel arrangement would be 0-22-0!   Jamie Squibbs

'57' PORTFOLIO

57004 + 57009 *(above) make their way out of Sheerness across the marshes on 27th July with 6Z74, Sheerness - Hitchin, empty scrap. This is the first time in 2010 Class 57s have been used on this service and it is commendable that DRS have decided to make more use of their 'heritage' fleet of loco!*   Stuart Chapman

Three months earlier, '004 + '009 were out again, this time on 16th April, working an Anglo-Scottish intermodal, 4M82, Coatbridge - Daventry. On a glorious Spring day, Nos.57004 + 57009 (below) pass Hardington Farm, Lamington, in the Upper Clyde Valley, with a well loaded train. The meandering waters of the infant River Clyde can be seen to the right of the leading Class 57 loco.   Guy Houston

57009 + 57003 *(above) form a different pairing on 11th April, allocated to 4M71, Tilbury - Daventry, 'Sugarliner'. The train is passing through a cutting at Brington on the 'Northampton Loop', which is an important freight artery, which relieves the pressure on the two-track section of the WCML between Roade and Rugby.* Richard Denny

57011 *(below) represents the new order as DRS switch from '66/4' to '57' traction on the Grangemouth - Aberdeen intermodal services (4A13 and 4N83) with effect 9th August. Two days later, as the sun begins to set, shadows lengthen and a beautiful autumnal glint greets the eye, as No.57011 passes Elliot Junction, Arbroath, on 4N83, Craiginches - Grangemouth.* Jim Ramsay

133

57601 - Royal Scotsman Manoeuvres

The Royal Scotsman makes a surprise and rare visit to Stirling for stabling on 17th August during a golf tour of Scotland for some wealthy individuals, who had been dropped off at Gleneagles, before the train ran ECS to Stirling and back to Perth. However, it's the magnificent semaphores which really steal the show in these two images.

Having run round, No.57601 (above) is seen leaving the loop by Stirling 'Middle' signal box with 5Z87 ECS and then (below) entering Stirling station. No.57601 is the prototype ETS loco, rebuilt in 2001, whose specifications are the same as a Class 57/0. As can be seen, No.57601 wears a LMS - Red style livery, officially WCRC Maroon, albeit with a black bodyside stripe. Guy Houston (2)

57604

Resplendent and gleaming in Brunswick Green livery, No.57604 'Pendennis Castle' (above) leads 1C99, the 23:45 London Paddington - Penzance, 'Night Riviera' on 3rd July at Trerulefoot, near Liskeard. This loco has been repainted to mark the 175th anniversary of the Great Western Railway, leaving Nos.57602 and 57605 in FGW Blue, whilst No.57603 retains the old style FGW livery of Green with gold stripe. Jamie Squibbs

Here we go again, same location, exactly one year after photographing the 37's on (supposedly) the last loco-hauled 2072, Bristol Temple Meads - Weymouth. Today, 4th September, the same Summer Saturday train is hauled by No.57604 'Pendennis Castle' (below), complete with 'Sand and Cycle Explorer Weymouth' headboard. The train is seen passing near Yarnbrook, just north of Westbury. Steven King

59201 *'Vale of York'* (above) is seen on the low level lines at Warrington on 3rd March with 6F38, the 06:50 Fiddlers Ferry - Liverpool Bulk terminal, HTA empties en-route to Latchford Sidings for a reversal. DBS are persevering with Class 59/2s on heavy coal and petroleum flows on otherwise Class 60-hauled flows.   Fred Kerr

59205 *'L. Keith McNair'* (above) makes for a striking composition on 11th March, working flat out at Margam Moors in charge of the loaded 6B13, Robeston - Westerleigh. Class 66/0 No.66067 is tucked-in behind 'DIT' as insurance in case of any problems - this being third time lucky for a successful run with a 59/2!   Mark Thomas

59206 *'John F. Yeoman Rail Pioneer'* (above) is also seen on 3rd March, passing Arpley Junction, Warrington, with 6F74, the 12:11 ex-Liverpool Bulk Terminal, loaded HTAs. This loco was the first to carry the DBS livery - a version of the German 'Pillar Box' or 'Traffic' red & grey colour scheme. Fred Kerr

59203 *'Vale of Pickering'* (above) runs solo on 1st April with a shortened rake of TEA and TDA loaded petroleum tanks, forming 6B13, Robeston - Westerleigh, and is descending from Bishton Flyover onto the South Wales Main Line. Note the truncated number '03' on the front of the loco. Jamie Squibbs

Fastline Coal Obituary
12th May 2008
to
25th March 2010

Fastline entered the coal market with a small fleet of Class 66/3s, adorned in grey & black livery with white & orange stripes. The initial contract involved moving coal from Daw Mill colliery to E.on's power station at Ratcliffe-on-Sour in the East Midlands.

To begin with, services were rather hybrid as only a handful of new '66/3s' and IIA coal hoppers were ready for use. So, train sets were formed of 'spare' GBRf HYA wagons and 'hired in' DRS Class 66/4 and GBRf Class 66/7 locos.

As Fastline's sphere of operations grew, as well as coal loaded at Daw Mill and Hatfield Mine, the Company also moved imported coal from Avonmouth, Immingham, Liverpool and Portbury, all of which was destined for Ratcliffe and Ironbridge power stations.

To mark the passing of Fastline's brief excursion into the coal sector, here are three images of their Class 66/3s at work on the rarely photographed Ironbridge power station circuit.

During 2009, Fastline was awarded a contract to deliver imported coal from Immingham to Ironbridge power station. In the early morning mist of 11th March, No.66305 (top) is on the final few yards to Madeley Junction with 6G30, the 05:45hrs ex-Liverpool BT, and is passing a warning sign advising drivers of a 'poor adhesion site'.

On 24th June 2009, No.66302 (above) is seen in late evening summer sunshine with 6Z15 ex-Immingham, passing the former Coalbrookdale station, which is now the home of the Green Wood Trust.

On 2nd March, No.66303 (opposite) runs past Shifnal returning with empty coal hoppers, running as 4D30, Ironbridge - Liverpool Bulk Terminal. Mike Hemming (3)

59002 *'Alan J. Day'*

(Left)

After a ballast drop and a visit from a weed-killing MPV, the line to Tytherington Quarry (South Glos.) sees several trainloads of inward stone scalpings in August from Whatley using JNA and JYA box wagons. The stone is then blended for road distribution from the quarry.

No.59002 simmers away on the branch at Latteridge crossing, with 7Z53, the 11:50 empties to Whatley. This is the first time in two years that stone workings have been seen on the branch! **Richard Giles**

66161

(Centre)

On 21st April, due to the failure of WSMR Class 67 No.67010, DBS Class 66/0 No.66161 is called upon to 'drag' 1P01, the 05:42 Wrexham - Marylebone, from Bescot Goods Loop to Birmingham International.

Upon arrival at Birmingham International, running about two hours late, passengers detrain and the set heads back ECS to Bescot.

David Weake

66612 *'Forth Raider'*

(Left)

For the past five years, No.66612 has been running around the network without Freightliner branding on its bodysides (See 'Railfreight Yearbook 2005') and is still doing so in 2010!

On Friday, 23rd April, the unbranded Class 66/6 is seen passing through Nether Booth, Edale, in the beautiful Peak District with 6Z39, Dowlow - Luton; a cloud of dust being thrown up in its wake from the MJAs filled to the brim with Limestone. **Ian Ball**

66522

(Right)

This is an interesting vantage point on the Cheltenham - Birmingham line.

On 28th March, 'Shanks' No.66522 emerges from the north portal of Church Road Tunnel, near Five Ways, with an engineers train, running as 6Y26, Standish Jct - Bescot.

The railway runs parallel with the Worcester & Birmingham Canal here, which climbs over 400ft. on its journey from Worcester to Birmingham.

Apart from engineers trains, such as this, no 'booked' freight is otherwise routed this way. David Weake

66703 *'Doncaster PSB'*

(Centre)

This image illustrates the new sidings at Long Lyes, Kilmarnock, on the G&SWR. This is where empty coal trains from the south will reverse before retracing their steps to gain access to the coal loading point at New Cumnock. No.66703 pulls into the new sidings on 20th May with 4S51, Drax - New Cumnock.

If a new crossover was to be installed at New Cumnock, this would eliminate a time consuming round trip to Kilmarnock, in the region of 45 miles. Max Fowler

66412

(Right)

On 4th April, DRS 'Malcolm' Class 66/4 No.66412 sits in Bedford St John's Goods Loop coupled up to WCRC's 'travelling billboard' Class 47/4 No.47826, with ECS prior to running round and working 5Z44, the 11.55 Bedford - Carnforth.

Nos.47826 and 47786 failed at Scarborough the previous day before working a return charter to Bedford. WCRC then acquired No.66412 from York and the '66' assisted the 47's back to Bedford throughout! Nigel Gibbs

66152 This image is very reminiscent of 'Speedlink', where the consist comprises a mix of wagons. Now under DBS 'Wagonload' management, Class 66/0 No.66152 (above) passes Banbury North signal box on 17th May with 6V03, Kineton - Didcot Yard, MOD service. Steven King

No.66152 (below) is seen passing Broughton Gifford on the 8m 30ch single line, which links Thingley Junction on the Paddington - Bristol main line and Bradford Junction on the Bath - Westbury line. The train - 6Z41, the 13:50 Newport ADJ to Westbury - is being diverted via Swindon on 4th March as the train includes some ISO tanks, which are not permitted via the usual route under Dundass Aqueduct in the Avon valley. Kevin Poole

Moving onto Southern Region metals, No.66152 (above) passes through Shortlands on 8th April with MBA 'Monster' box wagons loaded with scrap metal, running as 6O65, Willesden - Sheerness. At Shortlands, the lines merge from Nunhead and Beckenham Junction. Richard A. Jones

Harrowden Junction, Wellingborough, was remodelled in 2009. On 9th July No.66152 (below) is seen at the junction coming onto the main line off the bi-directional 'slow' line with 6E93, St.Pancras - Peterborough, empty cement tanks, 4 hours late. Sometimes, this stock will go to the Castle Cement plant at Clitheroe on a Friday to form 6Z73, the 13:50 (SO) Clitheroe - Leicester, cement. Richard Denny

66086 + 66157 *(above) represent the new order, as DBS persevere with 2 x Class 66/0 power on heavy petroleum trains emanating from Robeston and so reducing their dependence on Class 60s. On 9th February, as storm clouds gather, Nos.66086 + 66157 double-head 6B33, Theale - Robeston, empty bogie tanks, heading west along the embankment at Knighton, near Uffington, in the Vale of the White Horse.* Martin Buck

66707 *'Sir Sam Fay GREAT CENTRAL RAILWAY'*

On the first working, No.66707 is waiting at the exit signal to draw out, propel back, run round and depart Forders Sidings, via Bletchley, with 6O36, the 09:05 Forders - East Grinstead. The loco is returning MLA wagons to East Grinstead on 6th July, in connection with removing spoil from the Bluebell Railway. Forders Sidings actually closed last year but re-opens for this traffic! Nigel Gibbs

66434 *(above) is acquired by Colas Rail following the demise of Fastline in March, but still retains their striking colour scheme. Here, the photographer manages to obtain a good photograph of No.66434 as it passes through Carlisle Citadel station on 8th April with 6J19, Carlisle Yard - Chirk, loaded timber. Bear in mind the train was moving at the time and there was no flash!* Kevin Poole

66414 'James the Engine'

Poor old 'James' looks somewhat forlorn and out of place now that DRS have lost the 'Tesco Express' contract to DBS. Here, the Stobart-branded loco (above) is seen top 'n' tailed with Compass branded No.66417 passing Wandel Mill, north of Abington on 15th April with 6M50, (ThO) Torness - Carlisle, which has a payload of two Magnox flasks on this occasion. Keith McGovern

59206 *'John F. Yeoman Rail Pioneer'*

Built : 1995

Operator : National Power

Original Name : *'Pride of Ferrybridge'*

Transferred : 1998

New Operator : EWS (now DBS)

Re-liveried : 2009

Re-named : *'John F. Yeoman Rail Pioneer'*

DBS continue to try other traction as substitute motive power for Class 60s on Robeston oil trains. On 28th July, No.59206 (above) is seen crossing the footpath at the end of its journey down the Westerleigh branch with 6B13 loaded bogie tanks. Dave Gower
It had to happen, didn't it?

While 'outbased' at Margam, a Class 59 would eventually drop onto a non-petroleum train and, on 1st August, it does happen. No.59206 is allocated to 6B11, Margam - Trostre, and 6B64 return. The '59/2' (below) is seen coming off the Corus line with 6B64 and rejoins the national network at Genwen Junction. Mark Thomas

No.66845 (above) is seen on 21st May hauling 7Z98, the 04:48 Dollands Moor - Dagenham Dock, 'Blue Train' and travelling east along the former Tottenham & Hampstead Junction Line, having passed under the ECML and approaching Harringay Green Lanes.   Nigel Gibbs

This view of No.66845 (below) shows the Colas Rail logo applied underneath the cab window and, whilst there is no other Colas branding, the former DRS Compass logo has been removed. The loco is seen at Paddock Wood on 17th July at the head of a very late running 4Z92, 18:50 (MWFO) Hams Hall - Dollands Moor, intermodal destined for Novara in Italy.   Ian Cuthbertson

66845	
Ownership Details	
Leased	: 2003
Operator	: DRS
Original No.	: 66410
Transferred	: 2009
New Operator	: Colas Rail
New Number	: 66845

67018 'Keith Heller'

(Left)

The Maple-Leaf 'Skip' finds itself North of the Border having a stint on the Edinburgh 'Bins'.

Although it has worked the service on numerous occasions, this is its first working and, unfortunately, on a day when the weather is foul!

On Saturday, 27th February, No.67018 is passing Inveresk, near Monktonhall Junction, with 6B44 empty domestic waste containers, returning from Oxwellmains to Powderhall.

Keith McGovern

66110

(Centre)

Weekend engineering work on the main line between Port Talbot and Bridgend often results in diversions via Tondu.

On 12th September 2009, 6H25, the 09:56 Margam - Llanwern, steel arrives at Tondu in the former GWR Ogmore Valley sidings behind No.66110, seen amidst some excellent GWR lower quadrant semaphores.

Operationally, 6H25 is top 'n' tailed and No.66143 (out of view) will take the train back out towards Bridgend. Dave Gower

66403

(Left)

Following the previous transfer in July 2009 of 'off lease' ex-DRS Class 66/4s No.66401 and No.66402, No.66403 now joins the GBRf GBCM Loco Pool.

In this view, No.66403 is seen on 18th March away from its usual infrastructure duties in the South East, having arrived at Hams Hall with 4M23 intermodal ex-Felixstowe, substituting for the 'booked' Class 66/7 loco.

David Weake

66709 *'Joseph Arnold Davies'* (above) is involved in a bizarre translator vehicle movement on 10th September which also features three other locos in the consist. Running as 5Y66, Eastleigh - St Leonards Train Care Depot, the 'Medite' '66/7' hauls 'Translators' No.ADB975875 and No.ADB977087 + No.73207 + No.66401 + No.73212, photographed coming down Polhill.   Alan Hazelden

66434 (above) still retains the striking Fastline colour scheme and branding, despite being part of the DRS fleet, XHIM Pool, since March. On 17th September, No.66434 makes a surprise appearance on 4M71, the 10:53 Tilbury - Daventry, 'Sugar Liner' and is seen passing Chelmscote on the WCML, south of Bletchley. The train is conveying Tate & Lyle branded ISO tanks.   Nigel Gibbs

When not involved on charter work, the Class 'fill-in' on freight 'trips' from time to time, as on 4th November 2009 when Nos.67016 + 67027 (above) are allocated to the Arpley - Blackburn trip. On a fowl day, the pair approach Euxton on the return 6F43, Blackburn - Warrington Arpley, wagonload service.   Fred Kerr

WSMR / Chiltern take delivery of another Ruston & Hornsby shunting loco on 9th July for use within Wembley LMD. It is a 0-6-0, built in June 1961, originally based at Bramley CAD, Hampshire, carrying Army Nos.AD423 and 8217 during its life. It is collected from the old water terminal sidings near Neasden South Junction in a special move by WSMR Class 67 No.67010; dispensation for this move is required as the loco is not Network Rail registered. No.67010 (below), with the Ruston shunting loco in tow, is seen having crossed the 'Up' line into Marylebone and is about to cross the points onto the 'Down'.   Geoff Plumb

Normally, this is a Class 92 turn but, on 5th February, 6A42, Daventry - Wembley, is entrusted to Class 67 No.67029 'Royal Diamond' (above) which is seen passing Gordons Lodge on the Northamptonshire-Buckinghamshire border heading south with the empty vans, which had previously taken French bottled water to DIRFT.   Richard Denny

67018 '**Keith Heller**' *is named to honour the co-Chairman of DBS. As mentioned before, the loco is personalised with a large maple leaf, to recognise Mr Heller's Canadian nationality and is painted in the Canadian National colours. On 18th February, due to problems with No.67015, WSMR hire-in No.67018 (below), which is seen here running adjacent to the elevated section of the M6 Motorway on the approach to Bescot station with 1P13, the 11:10 Wrexham - London Marylebone.*   David Weake

Clitheroe Cement

The Castle Cement flow (6S00 loaded / 6M00 empty), introduced in 2008, has been a welcome addition to freight services on the 'S & C', providing numerous photographic opportunities; No.66099 (above) heads across Ribblehead viaduct with 6S00, Clitheroe - Mossend, loaded Cement tanks on 12th April against a backdrop of Park Fell, Simon Fell and Ingleborough. The setting sun shows off the arches to good effect.   Dave Gower

Not only do DBS have a good selection of wagons vandalised by graffiti, they now have a 'shed' as well. As you can see, No.66099 (below) carries the scars on the lower body side, as it climbs over Sheriff Brow viaduct, Stainforth, on 23rd July with 6S00 to Mossend.   Richard Armstrong

Truly stunning .... the Settle & Carlisle in all its glory! Running slightly early due to only having a short consist of loaded cement wagons, a rather clean No.66139 (above) drops down through Birkett in superb evening light on 26th April with 6S00, the 17:05 Clitheroe - Mossend.　　　　　　　　　　　　　　　Richard Armstrong

Prior to working 6S00 (top left) later in the day, No.66099 (below) is seen for the third time in this portfolio with the inward empty JPA cement tanks crossing Denthead viaduct, running as 4M00, (TX) Mossend - Clitheroe. There are some splendid architectural structures on the 'S & C' and four can be seen in a 10-mile stretch between Ribblehead and Garsdale; Blea Moor Tunnel (1m 869yds long), Ribblehead, Denthead and Arten Gill viaducts, at 440yds, 199yds and 220yds long, respectively.　　　　　　　　　　　　Dave Gower

Location, Location, Location …. is so important and, if you get it right, the train is almost secondary when it comes to good composition. With a splendid backdrop of giant dockside cranes, Freightliner's No.66505 (above) snakes its way out of Felixstowe with train 4R97 to Tilbury on 5th June and will join the branch at Trimley. Note the fixed distant on the left, quaint that a fish tail semaphore is still used!

Moving into Scotland and onto the Highland Main Line, Class 66/0 No.66116 (below) is on 4D47, Inverness - Mossend, 'Stobart' intermodal and approaches Whitehall User Worked Crossing (UWC) in the Pass of Drumochter on 5th June, climbing to the summit, thence the long descent to Blair Atholl and Pitlochry.

Nick Slocombe (2)

Tunnel Vision

The sides of the cutting have been cleared by Network Rail and a clear view is afforded of the split level lines which run to Patchway 'Old' and 'New' Tunnel, respectively. On 15th June, No.66060 (above) is seen leaving the 'New' Tunnel with a Wagonload service of cars, running as 6V51, TThO Warrington - Portbury. Dave Gower

The area above the north portal of Harbury Tunnel has been cleared of vegetation, presumably to prevent landslip. On 19th July, DBS Class 66/0 No.66183 (below) emerges into the tree-lined cutting with 6E55, Theale - Lindsey, empty petroleum tanks. Nick Slocombe

The Long Drag

Colas Rail No.66843 (above) approaches the summit of the Settle and Carlisle at Ais Gill on 14th April with 6J37, Carlisle Yard - Chirk, loaded timber for the Kronospan works. At this time, this working normally uses the WCML route via Penrith, but is going S&C for route learning for Colas drivers.

Class 66s are so quiet, this one nearly catches the photographer out, despite being on full power and working up the steep gradient. Fortunately, FHH No.66618 (below) is only doing around 30mph as it passes Smardale, Kirkby Stephen, heading a loaded 6E73, Killoch - Ferrybridge, coal train, also on 14th April. Stephen Dance (2)

GOLDEN OCHRE

The DBS Class 66/0s may be disliked by many enthusiasts, but they can form the basis of some excellent compositions, as this and the image below demonstrate. Here, No.66126 (above) is silhouetted against the sunset, passing Renishaw on the 'Old Road' between Chesterfield and Rotherham, on 12th August with 6Z44, Shipley - Cardiff Tidal, scrap metal service. The sun actually sets 20 minutes previously, but the photographer manages to get the very last of the colour, one minute later and it has all gone!   Mick Tindall

The valley lines in South Wales attract little photographic attention these days, due to the fact there is little freight activity and, what freight there is, is in the hands of a 'shed'. However, this is image provides a beautiful vista. On the Cwmbargoed branch, No.66164 passes Trelewis on 27th October 2009 with 6C93, the 13:00 Cwmbargoed - Aberthaw, loaded HTAs. The branch runs as a 'freight only' single line for some seven miles from the main line at Ystrad Mynach.   Dave Gower

First & Last 'Cans'
86637 & 86622

In June, Freightliner unveil the first member of their pre-'Powerhaul' fleet to receive their new livery, recently applied to the Company's new Class 70s.

Class 86/6 No.86637 has the honour and is re-painted in the new design of streamlined curves, with the addition of the colour silver, but retaining Freightliner's distinctive yellow and green colours and branding.

The rest of the fleet will be re-liveried and means that Class 86/6 No.86622 is the sole remaining member of the Class to carry the original two-tone grey livery. The Class 90 fleet will also be re-liveried and No.90045 is the first 'Skoda' to carry the new livery, followed by No.90049, so leaving just five of the Class to follow suit (Nos. 90042 / 043 / 044 / 047 and 048), not including long-stored No.90050.

The sole Class 86/6 in two-tone grey, No.86622 (top), is the second loco of 4L92, the 14:03 Ditton - Felixstowe, paired with No.86614. It is seen passing through Highbury & Islington on 24th June about to disappear into the darkness, studiously ignored by two passengers looking for the next westbound LOROL train.   Nick Slocombe

It's 23rd June and the first time No.86637 (above) leads a service in daylight hours since its repaint, and very smart it looks too... paired with No.86632, the 'celeb' passes Althorp Park, between Harlestone and Great Brington on the 'Northampton Loop', whilst in charge of 4M54, the 10:28 Tilbury - Basford Hall, freightliner.   Richard Denny

'ED' Gallery

The Class 73 Electro-Diesels are a firm favourite, now over 40-years old, and still providing sterling service, mostly on infrastructure trains around the south east of England. Here are a few images which caught my eye! Firstly, on 30th January, traction for 6G10, Dartford Junction - Hoo Junction, engineers train is a combination of owner-liveries; ex-Network Rail yellow No.73212 + First GBRf No.73141 'Charlotte' (above) pass Milton Range, close to their destination. The electricity pylons are certainly over-powering here! Ian Cuthbertson

(OVERLEAF)

Page 162:

73206 'Lisa' + 73213 *(top) look like they are backing on to an intermodal train in Eastleigh Yard on 7th February, but it's an optical illusion, they are merely running into the yard light engine.* Simon Howard

73201 'Broadlands' *(bottom) in striking BR Blue livery, passes Egham (between Staines and Virginia Water) on 30th January with an ECS move formed of five ex-Virgin liveried Mk2 air-conditioned vehicles, running as 5Z73, Selhurst - Eastleigh; a low Winter sun helps accentuate the colourful consist.* Jamie Squibbs

Page 163:

73141 'Charlotte' + 73212 *(top) in First Group indigo blue with pink & white stripes livery, top 'n' tail 1Q62, Selhurst - Selhurst, test train on 3rd June. The train is passing Dollands Moor, having left the 'Down Main' at Saltwood Junction and on to the 'Down Dover', now heads towards Folkestone and Dover priory.* Edward Clarkson

73141 'Charlotte' + 73213 *(bottom) along with sister 'ED' No.73206 'Lisa' (DOR) take ex-DRS Class 66/4 No.66410 from Hastings to London, as 5Z73, St. Leonards - Willesden Brent. The train, inclusive of two barrier coaches, heads through Kensington Olympia on the 'Down West London' line, on 24th February.* Ian Cuthbertson

73206 *'Lisa'* + 73213   73201 *'Broadlands'* ▼

▲ **73141** *'Charlotte'* **+ 73212**　　　　　　　　**73141** *'Charlotte'* **+ 73213** ▼

73107

'Spitfire' (above) climbs Upton Scudamore Bank at Old Dilton, with Class 31 No.31233 pushing from the rear, on a 1Q10, Westbury - Eastleigh, Serco test train - 21st April - a sight the photographer never thought he would see in this neck of the woods - just goes to show you can never rule out the unexpected!   Kevin Poole

'Redhill 1844 - 1994' (below) loses its 'Spitfire' nameplates, reverting to 'Redhill 1844-1994' while at St. Leonards on the 9th September. On 22nd September, It charges through Gatwick Airport with 1Q69, Three Bridges - Selhurst, having visited the south coast and now on its way back via East Croydon and Caterham. Network Rail Class 31/6 No.31602 'Driver Dave Green' tails the '69' special!   Nick Slocombe

73138 *(above) returns to traffic, modified with additional lights and a camera at one end. On 28th August, it hauls 1Q62, the 09:00 Hither Green - Selhurst, (No.31233 tailing) through Abbey Wood on the North Kent Line; Canary Wharf Tower in London's Docklands is clearly visible on the skyline.* Richard A. Jones

73213 *(overleaf) is heading 'The Caterham Corps' multi-leg (1Z82 - 1Z92) jaunt from Hastings on 10th October 2009 visiting lines in the London suburbs, featuring Hastings Line DEMU No.1001. The colourful ensemble passes Bexley with leg 1Z84, the 10:53 Bromley - London Bridge, via Slade Green.* Ian Cuthbertson (2)

73208 **'Kirsten'** **+ 73141** *(below) in BR Blue and First Group Indigo Blue with Pink & White stripes, respectively, pass Gravesend on 10th April with HQA Autoballasters, running as 6G14, Headcorn - Hoo Junction.*

92043 *'Debussy'* (above) is one of several '92s' carrying Europorte branding, which is a Company composed of the French branch of Veolia Cargo (acquired by Eurotunnel at the end of November 2009), Europorte 2 and GB Railfreight (acquired from FirstGroup at the beginning of June). No.92034 is seen emerging from the tree lined cutting at Polhill with 6Z93, the 11:25 Dollands Moor - Willesden, GBRF crew training run on 3th September. The train is formed of MRA Bogie Side Tipping Ballast Wagons.

At the time of this image, here is a snapshot of the 'Pool' allocations for the Class 92s showing on TOPS:

WTAE : 92001 / 003 / 005 / 007 / 009 / 012 / 017 / 019 / 022 / 026 / 034 / 037 / 042

GBET : 92028 / 032 / 038 / 043 / 044

92009 *'Elgar'* (previous page) is elegance personified, showing off the classic lines of the AC / DC loco. In this view, No.92009 is hauling a rare daylight working on 10th July, 6O63, Warrington - Dollands Moor, China Clay empties. The train would normally pass through Kent late on Friday, but handily runs on the Saturday morning, the sun shining down, as it heads through Kemsing on the Otford - Maidstone East line. Alan Hazelden (2)

92017 *'Bart The Engine'* (above), the DBS Stobart Rail liveried Class 92, is seen away from its usual intermodal duties on the last day of 2009, leading an unidentified Warrington to Bescot Yard cartic train south through Norton Bridge on the relief line. An unidentified Virgin West Coast liveried Class 221 Super Voyager is heading north on the main, doing its best to obscure the train consist. *Jamie Squibbs*

90045 (below) becomes the first Class 90 to sport the new Freightliner colours and the smart looking 'Skoda' is seen heading north at Dudswell, near Berkhamsted, on 16th July with 4M81, Felixstowe - Ditton. Just to the right of the picture (out of view) is the Grand Union Canal, which runs parallel to the WCML here. *Ian Cuthbertson*

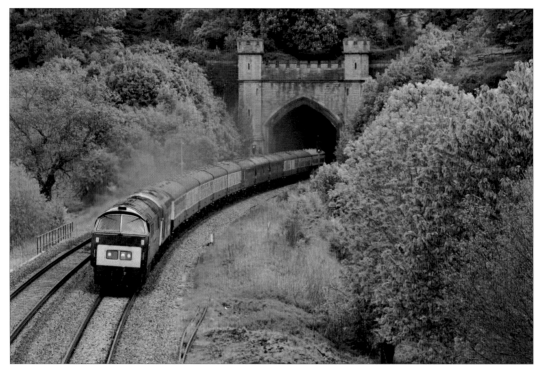

This rare event must surely rank as 'Railtour of the Year', when No.D1015 + No.40145 feature on the CFPS weekend excursion to Cornwall; 1Z40, the 05:20 Crewe - Penzance. On the outward journey, the Diesel Hyrdaulic and English Electric pairing are seen (above) powering out of Twerton Tunnel, Bath. D1015 is 'Western Champion', always has been and always will be, so why do people keep fiddling with the name - in this case, No.1015 is running with a 'Western Invader' nameplate on one side of the body and 'Western Firebrand' on the other - what purpose does this serve? Scott Turner

Three trains for the price of one and a rare occurrence at Taunton. On Saturday's outward journey, No.D1015 + No.40145 (above) head along the 'Down Main' and pass No.67005 'Queen's Messenger' on the VSOE, plus No.57308 'Tin Tin' sitting in the bay with the ECS off a service from Cardiff Central. Jamie Squibbs

On the return from Newquay to Par, No.1015 (opposite) leads the tour across Tregoss Moor, near Roche, which is the summit of this line. The location is the former A30 'skew road' overbridge, notorious for lorry strikes, but a nearby by-pass has now replaced this section of road. Richard Giles

D1015 + 40145

The East Lancs Champion

The weekend of 15th & 16th May sees the Class Forty Preservation Society run their ground-breaking tour involving diesel hydraulic Class 52 No.1015 'Western Champion' and Class 40 No.40145 'East Lancashire Railway' running to Cornwall, working in a combination of double-headed and top 'n' tail formations. The itinerary is as follows:

Saturday:

40145	:	Crewe - Winwick Jct - Earlestown - Eccles - Ordsall Lane - Manchester Victoria - Miles Platting - Ashton Moss North Jct - Denton Jct - Stockport - Cheadle Hulme - Macclesfield - Stoke on Trent - Norton Bridge - Stafford - Bushbury Jn - Bescot - Aston - Stechford - Birmingham International
D1015 & : **40145**		Birmingham International - Coventry - Kenilworth - Leamington Spa - Banbury - Oxford - Didcot North Jct - Foxhall Jn - Swindon - Chippenham - Bath Spa - Bristol Temple Meads - Taunton - Exeter St Davids - Newton Abbot - Plymouth
40145	:	Plymouth - Liskeard - Par - Truro - Camborne - St Erth - Penzance
D1015	:	Penzance - St Erth - Camborne - Truro
40145	:	Truro - Falmouth Docks
D1015	:	Falmouth Docks - Truro
40145	:	Truro - Camborne - St Erth - Penzance

Sunday:

D1015	:	Penzance - St Erth - St Ives
40145	:	St Ives - St Erth - Penzance
D1015	:	Penzance - St Erth - Camborne - Truro - Par
40145	:	Par - Newquay
D1015	:	Newquay - Par - Liskeard - Plymouth
D1015 & : **40145**		Plymouth - Bristol Temple Meads - Bristol Parkway - Swindon - Oxford
40145	:	Oxford - Crewe (reverse of outward route)

During the Easter weekend (Friday, 2nd April to Monday, 5th April) Pathfinder Tours run one of their 'Grand Scottish' railtours, involving the intrepid Class 40 No.40145 'East Lancashire Railway' *making a visit to the Kyle of Lochalsh, Fort William and Mallaig.*

On Sunday, 4th April, on the Kyle Line, No.40145 (above) passes through delightful Attadale with the Inverness - Kyle leg of the weekend charter and then, some 15 miles further into the journey, is seen again (below) crossing the bridge at Erbusaig, beneath which the Basa Dubh empties into Erbusaig Bay. The line speed ensures that several photographs can be obtained during No.40145's passage to the Kyle of Lochalsh. Jamie Squibbs (2)

40145
on the
'West Highlander'

Stranraer Steam - 10 years On

Apparently, the last time a steam train ventured to Stranraer was 10-years ago on 28th May 2000. The train should have been hauled by two 'Black Five' 4-6-0s, No.45407 (running as No.45157) and No.45110, which failed before the tour set out. Class 37 No.37405 was coupled inside No.45407 (No.45157) and worked throughout to Stranraer and back to Ayr, where No.37405 was removed and the solitary 'Black Five' worked the train from Ayr to Glasgow Central.

Stranraer is a remote place situated on Loch Ryan in the west of Dumfries & Galloway in the county of Wigtownshire, best known as a ferry port linking Scotland with Belfast, Northern Ireland. The line between Girvan and Stranraer has a very sparse passenger service, no freight, few charters and is under some threat, as it is proposed to move the ferries from Stranraer to a terminal some distance away on Loch Ryan. The railway will therefore lose any ferry passengers which it had.

On the fifth day of the 2010 'Great Britain III' tour (10th April), LMS Class 5MT 4-6-0 Nos.44871 + 45407 are allocated to work 1Z80, the 09:54 Glasgow Central - Stranraer, photographed north of Barrhill on a beautiful spring day. The 'Black 5s' (above) are negotiating the climb to the line's summit at MP16.5, which is an ascent of some nine miles or so at a ruling gradient of 1 in 67 out of Pinwherry. The train is allocated a time of over five hours to complete the 100-mile journey from Glasgow to Stranraer.   Donald Cameron

A Tribute to thy Greatness
(Overleaf)

Page 174: *These next two images are absolutely superb and illustrate what steam and heritage diesel traction both have to offer from a photographic perspective. There is no denying a full head of steam in a beautiful landscape is a dramatic combination and here, as part of the 'Great Britain III' charter, BR Britannia Class 7MT 4-6-2 Pacific No.70013 'Oliver Cromwell' and LNER K4 Class 2-6-0 No.61994 'The Great Marquess' are on the charge towards Drumochter Summit on 13th April with 1Z49, the 09:23 Inverness - Edinburgh. The two steam locos are working double-headed as far as Perth, from where No.70013 hauls the charter to Dundee with No.61994 on the rear. At Dundee, No.61994 is detached and No.70013 continues to Edinburgh.*   Jim Ramsay

Page 175: The return of 'Royal Scots Grey' *.... just like the good old days, the majestic sight of a 'Deltic' hauling a rake of blue & grey vehicles, albeit in this case a mix of Mk3s and Mk2E 'Air-Cons' heading across the Pennines. No.55022 looks imperious at the head of 1Z87, the 05:19 Stockport - Edinburgh Waverley, 'Deltic Retro II' charter, having emerged from Rise Hill Tunnel and is now approaching Garsdale. On the return journey, the charter takes No.55022 to its old stamping ground along the northern section of the East Coast Main Line - unfortunately, the weather is not as favourable as the outward journey. I know this image has been previously published in a monthly periodical, but it is worth making an exception.*   Richard Armstrong

'R.S.G.' Makes History

On Saturday, 18th September, Deltic No.55022 'Royal Scots Grey' makes, what is believed to be, the first visit by the Class into West Wales, as part of a Pathfinder Railtours excursion to Robeston and Fishguard Harbour. This portfolio celebrates the event.

'RSG' (above) is seen at Margam Knuckle Yard, having been detached temporarily from 1Z50 (ex-Crewe) in order to run-round the working; No.66015 taking the train forward due to issues with the run-round facility at Fishguard. Having visited the Robeston oil branch, 'RSG' (below) is seen coming off the Haverfordwest branch line with 1Z51, Robeston - Crewe, at Clarbeston Road, displaying the trademark 'Deltic' plume of exhaust.

'RSG' *(above) waits patiently at Fishguard Harbour to depart on the homeward run to Crewe. Following its departure, No.55022 (below) is then observed again (alas, for the last time here) some 50-miles further east, leaning into the curve alongside the sea wall at Ferryside, disturbing a flock of birds in the process.*

During the day, 'RSG' ends up working three legs of the charter: Crewe - Margam Knuckle Yard / Robeston - Clarbeston Road / Fishguard Harbour - Crewe. As previously reported, the charter is top 'n' tailed from Margam on the outward journey and DBS Class 66/0 No.66015 works the Margam - Robeston and Clarbeston Road - Fishguard Harbour legs - all in all, a great day for all concerned! Mark Thomas (4)

'Magnificent Seven to the Black Sea'

1st - 3rd May

Background: During the last three years, 17 Class 87s have been exported for use by BZK (the Bulgarian Railway Company) for use on freight traffic. There is still plenty of interest in the 87s and two other railtours have taken place in Bulgaria using 87s (No.87012 / October 2009 and No.87019 / October 2008), but this is the first to use them exclusively.

The PTG Raitour: Over the weekend of 1st - 3rd May, PTG organise the 'Magnificent Seven' charter, from Sofia (the Bulgarian Capital) to Varna on the Black Sea coast.

The tour details are:

Day 1 **BV3691** 09:40, Sofia - Kazanluk
  87003 Sofia - Pirdop
  87020 Pirdop - Kazanluk

BV3693 15:30, Kazanluk - Varna
  87020 Kazanluk - Razdelna
  87028 Razdelna - Varna

Day 2 **BV2690** 09:35, Varna - Shumen
  87028 Varna - Razdelna
  87004 Razdelna - Shumen

BV2692 13:30, Shumen - Resen
  87004 throughout

BV4691 16 :22, Resen - Veliko Turnovo
  87004 throughout

Day 3 **BV4693** 09:24, Veliko Turnovo - Gabrovo
  87004 throughout

BV3690 11:20, Gabrovo - Kazanluk
  87004 throughout

BV3692 14:55, Kazanluk - Sofia
  87004 Kazanluk - Pirdop
  87008 Pirdop - Sofia

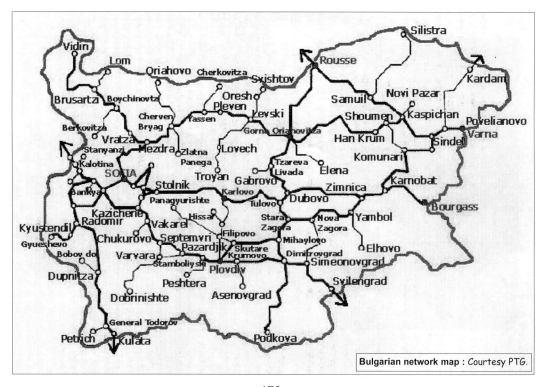

Bulgarian network map : *Courtesy PTG*.

Images : All images kindly provided by Richard A. Jones.

Above: *No.87004 'Britannia' pauses at Tryavna on 3rd May while working BV3690, the 11:20 Gabrovo - Kazanluk.*

OVERLEAF:

Page 180: *A particular favourite image .... No.87004 'Britannia' is seen running round 'The Magnificent Seven' at Gabrovo on 3rd May. The loco works in on BV4693, the 09:24 Veliko Turnova - Gabrovo and departs with BV3690 to Kazanluk*

Page 181: *A striking image of No.87003 as it pauses at Bunovo on day one, 1st May, with BV3691, the 09:40 Sofia - Kanaznluk. The '87' will work as far as Pirdop, where it will be replaced by No.87020.*

87003 (Left)

Day One:

Having worked the initial leg of the tour from Sofia, No.87003 comes off the train at Pirdop freight yard, replaced by No.87020.

There's just time to get that last photo as passengers start to rejoin the train for the journey to Kazanluk.

The train is BV3691, the 0940 Sofia - Kazanluk.

87004 (Centre)

Day Three:

During the lunch break, No.87004 'Britannia' pauses at Kazanluk, prior to departing at with BV3692, the 14:55 Kazanluk - Sofia.

No.87004 is the pride of the fleet and when BZK found out that this particular '87' had previously worked the Royal Train in Britain, the Company decided to allow the loco to retain its BR Blue livery and carry its original name.

Well done BZK!

87008 (Left)

Day Three:

On the same day, having reached Pirdop, the final loco change takes place and No.87004 hands over to Cotswold-Grey No.87008 for the first and only time.

No.'008 will have the privilege of hauling BV3692 the remaining 100kms back to the Bulgarian Capital, Sofia.

87028 (Right)

Day Two:

No.87028 hauls the first leg of day two - BV2690, the 09:35 Varna - Shumen, as far as Razdelna.

Here, it is seen about to be uncoupled from the train to allow No.87004 to take over for the remainder of the day.

87003 (Centre)

Day Three:

No.87003 has finished its tour duties for the weekend and is now seen stabled at Pirdop freight yard with Nos.87028 & 87019.

The three locos will remain here until their freight duties resume.

The three '87s' carry BZK Green & Yellow, DRS Blue and LNWR Black livery, respectively.

87033 (Right))

Day Three:

This particular loco along with No.87012 (in Network South East livery) stand at the head of two rakes of sulphuric acid tanks in Pirdop Yard.

Pirdop handles mainly non-ferrous metallurgic products from the nearby copper smelter and refinery, which is the biggest in South-Eastern Europe. The plant is owned by the German firm Aurubis and also produces Sulphuric Acid.

JANUARY 1960
The BRCW 'Cromptons'

Background

The British Rail Class 33 also known as the BRCW Type 3 or 'Crompton' is a 'Bo-Bo' Class of loco ordered in 1957 and built for the Southern Region of British Railways between 1960 and 1962. A total of 98 Class 33s were built by the Birmingham Railway Carriage and Wagon Company (BRCW) and were fitted with Crompton Parkinson electrical equipment installed in them. They were similar in appearance to their lower-powered BRCW sisters, the Scottish based Class 26 and Class 27s.

The original number sequence was D6500 - D6597 with Nos.D6500 - D6537 introduced in 1960 and the remaining members of the Class introduced in 1961 and 1962.

Their life began on the South-Eastern Division of the Southern Region and rapidly spread across the whole Region, many being used much further afield, as on the legendary Cliffe (Kent) to Uddingston (Glasgow) cement train, which saw a pair of locos work as far as York. Unfortunately, this service also gained notoriety when the derailment of a north-bound train resulted in the death of seven people and destroyed DP2, the Class 50 prototype, near Thirsk.

They were mixed traffic locos, but were all built with ETH (Electric Train Heating) supply and during the latter years were regular performers on Cardiff - Crewe and Cardiff / Bristol - Portsmouth Harbour passenger services. The Class survived until February 1997 when the remaining 17 Class members were withdrawn en-masse.

Sub-classes

There are three different types, later known as Class 33/0, 33/1 and 33/2.

This was a favourite location to photograph 'Cromptons' in 1990 - Lee station, just around the corner from Hither Green. Empty aggregate and tunnel segment trains had to traverse the very tight curve on Lee Spur Junction onto the Sidcup line and were therefore on full power once the end wagon had cleared the points. This gave some good audio entertainment and plenty of black smoke. This picture shows BR Blue-liveried Class 33/0s No.33023 + No.33006 (above) 'clagging' east with 6C66, the 10:02 Sevington - Cliffe Brent Marine empties on 25th May 1990.

Class 33/0: standard locos

The first locos were built as standard and, under TOPS, became Class 33/0 and numbered in the range 33001 - 33065 with two locos not surviving long enough to receive TOPS numbers. No.D6502 was withdrawn in 1964 after running through signals at Itchingfield, near Horsham, ramming the freight train ahead of it; the damage was so extensive it was cut up on site. This was followed by No.D6576 in 1968 after it was involved in a collision at Reading but, following recovery to Eastleigh, it was considered uneconomic to repair and cut up.

Class 33/1: 'Push - Pull' fitted

In 1966, D6580 (No.33119) was fitted with push - pull apparatus, high-level brake pipes and jumper cables to make it compatible with Multiple Unit stock. Tests were carried out on the Oxted Line using a rake of six unpowered multiple unit coaches. The use of this equipment removed the necessity for a loco to run round at a terminus station, as it could be controlled from the driving position of a Trailer unit and so could propel its train from the rear.

In 1968, following successful trials, D6580 and 18 others were likewise fitted and under TOPS became Nos.33101 - 33119. The main push-pull operations were trains running over non-electrified lines between Bournemouth and Weymouth, which operated like this for the best part of two decades. Weymouth trains started at London Waterloo powered by third-rail electric traction to Bournemouth, where the train would be divided with the 4REP remaining at Bournemouth station and the 4TCs hauled onward to Weymouth by a Class 33/1. On the return leg, the loco propels the train back to Bournemouth.

In later years, Weymouth 'Boat trains', conveying passengers from London for the Channel Islands, went over to Class 33/1 operation, albeit using conventional coaching stock initially. The route from Weymouth to the quayside is a tramway, following the harbour road, and as this line does not pass through Weymouth station, 'Boat Trains' could not call at Weymouth.

Class 33/2: narrow-bodied locomotives

The second batch of 12 locomotives were built with narrow bodies to allow them to work specific lines in Kent, notably the 'Hastings' line, which required the bodies to be reduced in width by seven inches to avoid hitting tunnel linings on that line - hence their nickname *'Slim Jims'*.

The 'Slim Jims' were numbered D6586 (33201) to D6597 (33212).

Class 33s today : Most of these locos have now been withdrawn from active duty and, at the time of writing, there are four examples remaining in traffic, whose details are:

Number	*Livery*	*Owner*	*Pool*	*Allocation*	*Name*
33025	WC	WCRC	MBDL	CS	Glen Falloch
33029	WC	WCRC	MBDL	CS	Glen Loy
33030	DRS	WCRC	MBDL	CS	
33207	WC	WCRC	MBDL	CS	Jim Martin

Images: To commemorate the 'Crompton's 50th Anniversary, I have included a small selection of photographs from the archive of:

Guest Photographer : **Peter Tandy**

Overleaf:

Page 186: *This is the Great Western Main Line at Acton on 19th July 1989 and Nos.33023 + 33020 double-heading 6V25, the (MO) 11:10 Halling - Greenford, loaded cement; a location now completely changed by Heathrow Express electrification paraphernalia and various building developments.*

Page 187: *On 13th April 1995, an unusual stock move takes place, taking a 4TC set from Derby to Ayr for a filming contract. As the stock had to be propelled, 2 x Class 33/1s were diagrammed for the job - Nos.33109 + 33116 being the locos selected. In the pleasant spring sunshine, standing on a footbridge just beyond Tutbury and Hatton station on the Derby - Stoke main line, the photographer captures the move for posterity. By the time the train appears, somewhat delayed, the sun is well round onto the front and makes for a super image.*

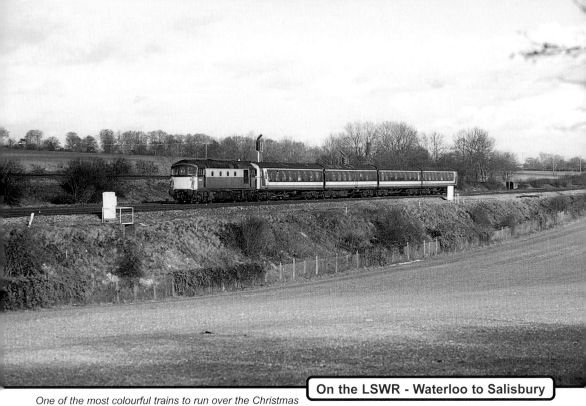

One of the most colourful trains to run over the Christmas holiday in 1990 was this one - No.33118 (above) in 'Dutch' civil engineers livery + NSE 4TC stock, forming the 12:15 Waterloo - Salisbury. It is pictured at Battledown, a few miles west of Basingstoke, where the lines to Salisbury and Winchester diverge. As a result of being fitted with 'Push-Pull' jumper cables, No.33118 will propel the train on the journey back to Waterloo.

Class 33/0 No.33012 (below) is seen at Salisbury on 4th April 1988 having arrived with ECS to later form an additional 18.00hrs departure to London Waterloo.

Class 50s arrive on the former London & South Western Railway route from London Waterloo - Exeter in 1980, but Class 33s could still be seen working trains 'vice' 50. On 27th December 1990, Class 33/1 No.33114 (above) leaves Woking with the 12:15 Waterloo - Salisbury, formed of Mk2 Network South East vehicles.

By August 1989 all workings from Exeter, Yeovil and Salisbury were diagrammed for Class 50s, but a 'Hoover' failure might result in a 'Crompton turning up. This is the case on 14th August 1989, when No.33113 (below) is called on to haul the 09:00 Yeovil Junction - Waterloo, pictured leaving Basingstoke and unusually crossing onto the 'Up Relief' line which means, in all probability, a slow journey behind a local EMU as far as Woking!

The West London Line — *Moving into London we come to Kensington Olympia on the afternoon of 30th March 1990 and see Hither Green allocated Nos.33056 'Burma Star' + 33042 (above) passing on a Park Royal - Angerstein Wharf train, which had earlier conveyed sea-dredged aggregate to the terminal. At this time, the platform by the train was not in public use; the semaphore signals have long gone and 3rd rail electrification is now in place.*

Just down the road , is Lillie Bridge depot of London Underground, where various battery locos can be seen 'on shed'. BR Blue Class 33/0 No.33058 (below) passes on the BR line on 30th July 1990 with the daily 7V20, Angerstein Wharf - Paddington, train of dredged sand. The extension to the Earls Court building can be seen in progress at the back of the train.

This photograph shows one of the first celebrity diesels repainted into an approximation of the original 1960s livery - No.33008 'Eastleigh' *(above)* - climbing Hatton Bank with a Poole - York relief service on 16th April 1987. The train was not booked to call at, and therefore reverse at Reading, travelling instead via Reading West Curve.

By the late 1980s there were occasional movements of army personnel from Wool in Hampshire to Birmingham New Street. On at least 2 occasions the train was formed of a class 33/1 and TC stock, which was the case on 17th June 1989 when No.33113 hauled two 4TC sets to England's 'Second' city. On the return, No.33113 *(below)* is seen in Harbury Cutting putting up a good show of exhaust as it nears the summit of the climb.

Construction Traffic

Wokingham in Berkshire did not see many freight trains in 1990, save for the eminently photographable 6O60, the 17:48 Theale - Northfleet, cement empties formed of 2-axle PCA tanks. This was a solid Class 33 turn, although it did go over to Class 60 haulage for a while before it stopped running. This image shows two Eastleigh allocated Class 33/0s - No.33009 + No.33029 (above) joining the Clapham Junction line on 25th May 1990.

Having just had a very heavy shower, evidenced by the black sky and puddles on the platform, Nos.33051 'Shakespeare Cliff' + No.33058 (below) enter Gravesend station on 26th October 1990 with loaded Foster Yeoman branded PGAs on an aggregate working from Grain to Sevington. Luckily, the sun appears just as the signal clears and the driver opens up the locos to give a nice smoke effect.

As part of major work to renovate Chatham Dockyard in 1991, contaminated spoil had to be removed from the site by rail via the short and steeply graded Dockyard branch. The majority of the workings were entrusted to Class 33s which, given the gradient of the branch and the weight of the train, were truly 'thrashed' as they worked up the branch to join the main line at Gillingham. Once these trains had left Chatham Dockyard branch they would run forward past Gillingham signal box in order to the clear the point work before setting back into the yard where the main line train was made up. No.33051 (above) is seen setting back into Gillingham yard, where three trainloads of spoil are joined together and then taken by a Construction Sector Class 56 to Forders Sidings for disposal.

Meanwhile, in 1989 there was a daily ballast working from Hoo Junction to Meldon quarry in Devon and here 'Slim Jim' Class 33/2 No.33211 (below) is seen passing Sidcup on 20th August 1989 with this working.

MARCH 1960

92220
'Evening Star'

The last steam loco:

Standard Class 9F No.92220 *'Evening Star'* was the last steam loco to be built by British Railways, completed in 1960 and the 999th loco of the whole British Railways Standard range.

Construction

Built at Swindon railway works, *'Evening Star'* is one of 251 9fs built, numbered 92200 - 92250, which has a 2-10-0 wheel arrangement. It is equipped with a BR1G-type tender and adorned in British Rail Brunswick green livery, normally the preserve of passenger locomotives, complete with a copper-capped double chimney.

All other members of the class of heavy freight locos were painted unlined black and No.92220 was the only Class 9f to be named when running with BR. The name *'Evening Star'* was chosen following a competition run by the Western Region Staff Magazine and a special commemorative plate was affixed below the nameplate on the smoke deflectors.

'Evening Star' also has the distinction of being the only British main line steam loco ear-marked for preservation from the date of construction.

In service

No.92220 was used on the Western Region and over the Somerset & Dorset Joint Railway line and on 8th September 1962 it hauled the last 'Pines Express'. It was withdrawn in 1965 after a working life of only five years!

In Preservation

For the most part, *'Evening Star'* has been a static exhibit at the NRM, York, before returning to its birthplace, Swindon Works, on 3rd September 2008.

When I was a Director of Pathfinder Tours, I always wanted to organise a tour to include both the last steam loco and last diesel loco to be built by British Rail. This came to fruition on 7th August 1988, when *'Evening Star'* and Class 50 diesel loco No.50037 *'Illustrious'* featured on 1Z46, the 05:52 Swindon - Scarborough, 'Yorkshire Venturer'.

'Evening Star' worked between York - Scarborough - Hull, while *'Illustrious'* hauled the outward leg from Swindon to York and the return from Hull. I believe this was No.92220's last run before its main line-running certifciate expired and it went to the National Rail Museum.

Top Right: *Resplendent in Brunswick Green livery, No.92220 awaits the off from Scarborough and the run down to Hull with 1Z46, the 16:20 Scarborough - Swindon.*

Bottom Right: *Some 23 miles further south, 1Z46 pauses at Bridlington for a 'photo-stop'.*

Top: *Nameplate and commemorative plate.*   Martin Buck (3)

Overleaf: Those were the days ....

Page 196: *No.92220 'Evening Star' has a tender full of coal ready for its next turn of duty at Cardiff Canton shed on 12th November 1961. This was No.92220's 'home' shed and she is seen in the presence of two 4-6-0 'Halls', No.6952 'Kimberley Hall' and No.4958 'Priory Hall'.*

Page 197: *Nostalgia indeed. A shabby and dirty looking No.92220 is approaching Bath (Green Park) on 15th August 1963 with the noon Templecombe - Bath; the return working of its first duty since being re-allocated to Bath in 1963.*

The Somerset and Dorset Railway completed its Bath extension in 1874, connecting into the Midland line at Bath Junction, half mile outside the station. Through trains running between the Midlands and South Coast had to reverse at Bath, the most famous of these being the 'Pines Express' from Manchester to Bournemouth West. Following the Beeching Report, passenger trains ceased from 1966, freight in 1971. In the 1980s, the rail approaches to Bath Green Park were redeveloped and the station itself pedestrianised. Hugh Ballantyne (2)

April 1960

Margam Marshalling Yard

Opening on 14th April 1960, Margam marshalling yard, near Port Talbot in South Wales, was heralded as the most modern in Europe, occupying 178 acres with 33 miles of track, 50 sidings, handling 3,000 wagons in an eight-hour shift. The yard also boasted in having the first retarder-fitted 'hump' yard on the Western Region.

A collection of 18 double-ended sidings eventually replaced the sprawling and decaying remnants of the original Margam Hump yard when the new centre for railfreight activity - Margam Traffic Centre - opened for business in November 1987. The new layout allowed access from two directions: the South Wales main line and direct from the nearby steelworks.

To facilitate the servicing of locos using the marshalling yard, Margam Depot (code 87B) was built on a landfill site and opened during March 1964. Consequently, Port Talbot Duffryn Yard closed and its allocation of Class 08 shunting locos (Nos.D3429 - D3438) were transferred, becoming Nos.08359 - 08368, respectively, under TOPS in 1974. No mainline locos have ever been allocated to Margam Depot.

During the 1970's, British Steel opened their Iron Ore terminal at Port Talbot Docks and Margam supplied several sets of 3 x Class 37s + 27 bogie tipplers (JTA / JUA) to convey Iron Ore to Llanwern Steel Works. These triple-headed Class 37s were an operational and maintenance nightmare for Margam and troublesome in getting them to work in multiple, together with modifications needed to strengthen the couplers.

By way of example, in 1987, a normal 24-hour period would see some 60 train movements at Margam, 50% of which would be steel traffic. However, over the years a continuing downturn in coal, oil, steel and wagonload traffic in West Wales has resulted in Margam TMD taking on work previously carried out by Landore, Llanelli, Pantyffynnon and Swansea East depot. Margam TMD officially closes in August 2009 and, with the earlier closure of Cardiff Canton, South Wales has no facility to undertake repairs and locos go to Toton TMD for repairs.

Fortunately, 50 years on, Margam yard is still going strong!

On 1st March, DBS Class 66/0 No.66020 (above) leaves Port Talbot slab terminal with 6H27, Port Talbot Field - Margam Knuckle Yard, formed of BAA bogie steel carriers, probably bound for Llanwern later in the day.

Shortly before the closure of Margam as a TMD, the photographer records this nocturnal scene of No.66112 (opposite) heading a line of Class 66/0s waiting another turn of duty.

Brush Bagnell shunting loco No.504 (below) enters Margam Knuckle Yard with a rake of loaded steel carriers to go back onto the national network, whilst sister loco No.501 brings a rake out of the yard in readiness for loading with more steel products. The two train sets have a selection of enclosed steel carrying bogie wagons, including steel sided IHAs and JSAs, both CAIB and VTG numbered varieties. Margam distributes trainloads of various steel products (mostly Slab and Hot Rolled Coil) to many destinations throughout the UK, such as Corby, Dee Marsh, Hartlepool, Llanwern, Round Oak and Trostre. Mark Thomas (3)

DECEMBER 1960

English Electric Type 3s

Background:

The British Rail English Electric Type 3 - Class 37 - is a diesel-electric loco ordered by British Rail as part of the 1955 Modernisation Plan, which was a result of indentifying a need for a number of mixed traffic type 3 locos of 1,500hp - 1,999 hp. English Electric had already been successful with orders for type 1 (Class 20) and type 4 (Class 40) diesels and had produced locos of similar power to that required for railways in East Africa.

Between, December 1960 - August 1965, a total of 309 locos were built at English Electric's Vulcan Foundry at Newton-le-Willows and Robert Stephenson & Hawthorns of Darlington, originally numbered in the range D6700 - D6999 and D6600 - D6608. The 37s are similar in appearance to the EE Class 40, albeit eight feet shorter in length, at 61ft 6ins. An initial batch of 30 locos (D6700 - D6729), were allocated to depots in the former Eastern Region:

Stratford (30A - 22 locos)   March (31B - 4)   Norwich (32A - 2)   Ipswich (32B - 2)

In common with most new diesel designs, the design incorporated a driving cab at each end of the loco and the fitting of under-slung equipment between the bogies, comprising a fuel tank and a boiler water tank for passenger steam-heating capability.

Initially, the first batches of locos had nose-end communication doors fitted, with a 2-digit headcode box mounted either side. It was intended for train crews to pass through these doors when locos worked in multiple or when train crew transferred between locos and coaches on long distance passenger runs. In practice, these doors were rarely used and from the batch No.D6818 - D6606, the doors were removed and a central headcode panel was fitted instead.

BR Duties:

The Class 37 became a familiar sight on many parts of the British Rail network, particularly in East Anglia, North East England, Scotland and South Wales, well-liked by enthusiasts, earning them the nickname, 'Growlers' or 'Tractors'.

Freight use was widespread, but passenger work less so, although they did see extensive use working out London Liverpool Street on the King's Lynn and Norwich routes. In the early 1980s the remaining steam-heat locos migrated to Scotland, replacing Class 27s on the West Highland Line and Class 26s on the Far North and Kyle lines. A notable exception saw 'freight-only' locos (usually operating in pairs) on the Cambrian Line on Summer-dated 'Saturday Only' trains from London / Birmingham to Aberystwyth and Pwllheli, taking over from Class 25s.

From 1985, Class 37/4s took over, replacing 37/0s in Scotland and on the Cambrian, plus Class 33s on the Crewe - Cardiff workings. Eventually, they lost their passenger work to 'Sprinters' and the like, although they did find work on the North Wales Coast and, until 2006, on DMU-replacement Cardiff - Rhymney services. The final daily work in Scotland was the Fort William sleeper train, which lost Class 37 traction in June 2006.

Their freight work similarly reduced, being displaced by higher powered locos, such as Class 56 and Class 58. Their real strength, however, was having a high 'Route Availability' (5) which means they can work almost anywhere on the rail network and this is one of the reasons you still find them working today, 50 years on!

TOPS Renumbering :

Renumbering of the Class 37 fleet under TOPS was straightforward with loco numbers remaining in sequence. So, for example, D6701 became No.37001, D6999 became No.37299, while D6600 - D6608 became Nos.37300 - 37308. The remaining exception, D6700, became No.37119 instead of D6819, which in turn became No.37283.

D6983 had been withdrawn in 1965 following collision damage and was thus excluded.

Rebuilding :

A number of locos were rebuilt as Class 37/9 in the late 1980s to evaluate Mirrlees and Ruston engines for possible use on a new Class 38 freight locomotive. These 'Slugs', as they were affectionately nicknamed, were heavily ballasted to improve traction and had excellent load-hauling capabilities. The Class 38 was never built.

Sub - Classes

In the 1980s, Class 37 locos were extensively refurbished and, as such, new numbers were allocated to reflect the modifications, thus:

Sub-Class	Description
37/0	Locos unmodified.
37/3	Locos re-bogied, but not refurbished.
37/4	Refurbished, rewired, English Electric generator replaced with Brush alternator, Electric Train Heating (ETH) fitted.
37/5	Refurbished, rewired, English Electric generator replaced with Brush alternator
37/6	Modified 37/5s, with through ETH wiring and RCH jumper cables.
37/7	Refurbished, rewired, English Electric generator replaced with GEC G564AZ or Brush alternator and additional weight added
37/9	Refurbished, rewired, English Electric generator replaced with Brush alternator. New Mirrlees MB275Tt or Ruston RK270Tt engines fitted.
Notes:	1. All refurbishment undertaken at Crewe, except for the Class 37/3s which had their bogies replaced at various depots.
	2. A loco carrying a number prefixed 37/8 is classified Class 37/7.

'LARGE LOGO'

In 1984 / 1985, a total of 31 Class 37s were overhauled, re-painted in 'large logo' (white double arrows) livery and fitted with Electric Train Heating (ETH). They became sub-class 37/4, numbered 37401 - 37431, and put to work on passenger services in South Wales, the West Highland Line and the lines in the far north of Scotland.

Along with Loadhaul black & orange, 'large logo' is one of the most aesthetically pleasing liveries to be carried by the Class, as this image will hopefully demonstrate. No.37427 (above) is seen away from its normal passenger duties, entering Newport station on 15th October 1986 with a rake of rusty-looking empty mineral wagons, running as 6A82, East Usk - Marine. No.37427 was named 'Bont Y Bermo' on 13th April 1986 at Barmouth.

Post - privatisation

Following refurbishment in the 1980s, the Class 37 fleet became one of the longest surviving classes on the railways but, with the introduction of new Class 66s, many '37s' have been withdrawn or scrapped. DB Schenker (ex-EWS) and Direct Rail Services (DRS) operate small fleets and some second-hand '37s' have been exported to France and Spain, allocated to infrastructure trains on the construction of high-speed rail links.

Network Rail ERTMS

Network Rail secure four Class 37s as part of the European Rail Traffic Management System (ERTMS) project on the Cambrian Line in 2008. They were overhauled at Barrow Hill, becoming essentially brand new, having been completely re-built and the cabs fitted with ERTMS signalling systems. The four '37s' are numbered 97301 - 97304 (ex-37100, 37170, 37178 and 37217, respectively) and are finished in Network Rail yellow livery.

Surviving 37s in Traffic

Out of the original 309 Class members, excluding those in preservation, here is a snapshot of the ones operated by DBS and DRS at 08:00hrs at the start of a new fiscal period, 6th April 2010:

	No.	Pool	Location	Working
DBS	37401	WKBN	Inverness	
	37425	WKBN	Aberdeen	
	37670	WFMU	Crewe	
DRS	37038	XHNC	Gresty Bridge	
	37059	XHNC	Norwich Crown Point	
	37069	XHNC	Derby RTC	
	37087	XHNC	Gresty Bridge	
	37194	XHNC	Crewe	6D41, Crewe - Valley
	37197	XHHP	Barrow Hill	
	37218	XHNC	Grangemouth	
	37229	XHNC	Crewe	6D41, Crewe - Valley
	37259	XHNC	Derby RTC	
	37261	XHSS	Eastleigh	
	37423	XHNC	Carlisle Kingmoor	
	37510	XHNC	Carlisle Kingmoor	
	37601	XHNC	Gresty Bridge	
	37602	XHSS	Carlisle Kingmoor	
	37603	XHNC	Gresty Bridge	
	37604	XHNC	Gresty Bridge	
	37605	XHSS	Eastleigh	
	37606	XHSS	Gresty Bridge	
	37607	XHNC	Carlisle Kingmoor	5Z20, Carlisle Kingmoor - Workington
	37608	XHNC	Crewe	6O62, Crewe - Dungeness (with No.20304)
	37609	XHNC	Crewe	
	37610	XHNC	Gresty Bridge	
	37611	XHNC	Gresty Bridge	
	37612	XHSS	Eastleigh	
	37667	XHNC	Carlisle Kingmoor	
	37682	XHHP	Barrow Hill	
	37688	XHNC	Crewe	

BARNETBY

I scheduled a trip to Barnetby in July 2001 to capture a 'cover shot' for the Winter 2002 edition of 'Freightmaster', notably the westbound 6D66, Immingham - Doncaster Belmont, 'Enterprise'. However, on the day, Class 37/6 No.37667 was allocated to work the outward leg (6D65) and this was too good an opportunity to let go. As No.37667 (opposite) slowly came into view, the peg went off on the 'Down Main' for 7C75, the 10:54 Immingham - Scunthorpe, loaded MGR. Although it seemed doomed to failure, I managed to record No.37667 just before Class 56 No.56064 did its best to obliterate the view. Superb action and one of my all-time favourites, although one enthusiast seems totally uninterested in the proceedings!

GREENHOLME

Along with Settle Junction, the West Coast Main Line at Greenholme in the Cumbrian fells is a favourite haunt of mine; a combination of beautiful scenery, tranquillity, disturbed only by the sound of a curlew overhead or the crescendo of an approaching freight tackling the ascent of Shap. Here, on 9th April 1997, ex-works, EW&S branded, Class 37/5 No.37503 (above) passes Greenholme with a departmental service bound for Carlisle. Nowadays, unfortunately, this view has been spoilt by additional electrification stanchions, which have been erected to help prevent the wires being brought down in strong winds.

Images

I have chosen a few images from my own modest archive to celebrate the 37's 'Golden Jubilee', all of which have some small story to impart. As you will see, several are 'portrait' orientation, a style for which I developed a liking. This was mostly due to necessity seeking out suitable photographs for the front cover of FREIGHTMASTER, which warranted this style of orientation.

FIRST ATTEMPTS

There now follows my first three photographs of Class 37s, dating back to May 1985 and May 1986, all featuring my favourite variant, the ones fitted with 'split box' reporting indicator panels. In the first scanned image, the focus of attention is the magnificent West Highland scenery and semaphore signals, which overshadow Class 37/0 No.37037 (below) awaiting departure time at Taynuilt with 1T28, the 13:00 Oban - Glasgow Queen Street.

Overleaf:

On 11th May 1985, while waiting for Class 27s, No.27054 + No.27206, to back onto our charter train (1Z86, the 09:33 Edinburgh - Oban), Class 37/0 No.37026 'Loch Awe' (page 206) accelerates past Cowlairs on the last leg of its journey, the train being 1T12, the 08:00 Oban - Glasgow Queen Street.

A striking view, well, in my opinion! Having received the single line token from the signalman at Crag Hall (Skinningrove) Nos.37064 + 37063 (page 207) continue on their way to the Boulby Potash mine on 11th May 1986 with a rake of empty covered hoppers, 'tripped' from either Middlesbrough Goods or Tees Dock.

The Burton 'Trip'

Following the arrival of EWS Class 66/0s, work for the venerable 37s grew less and less, restricted largely to local Enterprise 'trips', working off Warrington and Bescot, in particular. At the latter, there were out & back runs to Bloxwich, Bordesley, Longport, Walsall, and Burton-on-Trent / Toton; the latter is featured here.

At the time these photographs were taken, this diagram was booked for a Class 47 but, on 11th April 2002, No.37669 was turned out to work:

> *6P17, Bescot - Burton*
>
> *6D77, Burton - Toton*
>
> *6G77, Toton - Bescot*

The return working is ideal for moving wagons between the busy yards at Toton and Bescot, especially those going 'on' or 'off' repair. Here, No.37667 (above) hurries 6G77, Toton - Bescot, past Kingsbury comprising 2-axle TTA fuel oil tanks and bogie steel carriers - very reminiscent of 'Speedlink' days. Earlier, No.37667 (opposite) had arrived at Burton-on-Trent with 6P17 ex-Bescot and is busy shunting 2-axle SPA wagons loaded with steel wire before setting off with 6D77, Burton on Trent - Toton.

Newport

I made frequent trips to Newport, being one of the busiest places for freight on the network; the signals on the through lines changing from red to green every few minutes or so, heralding a constant flow of freight. Of course, in 1986, Severn Tunnel marshalling yard was still in use, Llanwern produced steel, Ebbw Vale tinplate and many Welsh pits were still mining coal. On 21st September 1986, Class 37/0 No.37222 (above) heads for Ebbw Vale with 4A84, Llanwern - Waunllwyd, loaded steel coil to be made into tinplate.

Meanwhile, heading in the same direction on 21st June 1995, coal - sector Class 37/7 No.37895 (below) is seen in charge of 6V07, the 09:50 Seaforth - Gwaun-Cae-Gurwen, empty 'Cawoods' FPA containers, which had previously run to Liverpool loaded with domestic coal bound for Ireland.

The bridge spanning the south end of Ebbw Junction was once one of the best photographic locations on the South Wales Main Line but now, like so many other locations around the country, our Health & Safety culture has resulted in high barricades being erected on the bridge, so preventing photography, unless of course you have a ladder in your pocket!

Back in June 2001, Transrail-liveried Class 37/4 No.47412 'Driver John Elliott' (above) is seen crossing from Ebbw Junction onto the main line in order to propel 6B50, Machen - Newport Alexandra Dock Junction, ballast into the yard. Due to run-round problems at Machen, these ballast trains were top 'n' tailed and No.37428 is on the rear of 6B50 (out of view) which had taken the empty wagons to Machen earlier in the day. In the background, two 'Enterprise' services are ready to depart: Nos.60094 + 60067 on 6M17, Newport ADJ - Wembley, plus an unidentified Class 66/0 on 6M75, Avonmouth - Warrington.

Ex-Mainline Class 37/0 No.37274 was renumbered No.37308 on 5th May 2000 and, following overhaul and repaint into BR Blue, allocated to Old Oak Common, WMOC - EWS Heritage Fleet. On 26th November 2002, No.37308 (above) is unexpectedly allocated to 6V38, Marchwood - Didcot, MoD service instead of the usual 'Shed' and, despite running very late, just manages to avoid the lengthening shadows, as it passes through Moreton Cutting with a mixed consist of army vehicles, containers and a single VGA van.

This '37' portfolio would not be complete without an image of a Loadhaul orange & black livery Class 37, one of the most striking liveries worn by the Class over the years. On 2nd August 1995, Class 37/7 No.37713 (below) passes Barnetby hauling two 2-axle crude oil TTAs and two TDAs, forming 6D99, the 08:40 TFO Immingham - Gainsborough.

My Home Patch

In the late 1980s, the daily 'feeder' service into the 'Speedlink' network at Gloucester was a solid '37' turn, running as 6B55, the 15:55 Swindon Cocklebury - Cardiff Tidal. It conveyed empty steel wagons from the Austin Rover factory, fuel oil tanks from the diesel stabling point and a private siding for Hartwell Oils, in Swindon, plus cement from Ketton.

On 10th September 1988, No.37197 (above) makes its way out of Swindon station with a short 6B55 heading for the Gloucester branch, at a time when there were several daily freight services on the 'Golden Valley' route between Swindon and Gloucester. On the branch itself, No.37232 (below) passes the emergency RAF Lyneham fuel dump at Purton, on the outskirts of Swindon, as it proceeds along the single line section. This runs for 12 miles from MP 78.20 at Swindon 'Loco Yard' to Kemble - the date is 23rd June 1988.

Great Western Railway
1825 - 2010

2010 marks the 175th anniversary of the creation of the Great Western Railway and a series of special events and steam excursions featuring GWR locos take place across the region to celebrate this milestone in railway history.

A small portfolio of images is included in this edition of Loco Review to celebrate the event.

Background: The Great Western Railway was created in 1835 and grew to be one of the largest and most well known railway companies in the world with a network radiating out of London to reach Penzance, South Wales and Merseyside.

Long before railways were thought of, merchandise was transported between the major ports of Bristol and London by way inland waterways - River Avon, Kennet & Avon Canal and the Thames - in the late 18th and early 19th centuries. However, canal transportation was costly and not very reliable in bad weather. The main road artery linking Bristol and London was the Bath Road; a popular stage coach route taking two days for passengers to travel between Bath and the capital. However, non-passenger traffic was slow and costly. Stage coaches were also subject to delay in bad weather, delaying the journey by hours, or even days.

However, the opening of the Stockton & Darlington Railway and the Liverpool & Manchester Railway in 1825 and 1830, respectively, changed things forever. In January 1833, a committee formed of several Bristol trading associations, including the Merchant Venturers and the Bristol Dock Company, met to discuss a new venture - to build a railway between Bristol and London.

The venture was given the go ahead and the first task was to select an engineer to survey the route and Isambard Kingdom Brunel, a mere 27 years of age, was chosen for the job. By July 1833, after Brunel started work, the Committee was in a position to obtain an Act for the construction of a line from Bristol to London via Swindon and Didcot. By 1835, sufficient capital had been raised to construct the line and on 31st August 1835 the Royal Assent to the Bill was given and the Great Western Railway was born .... the rest, as they say, is history.

SWINDON FLORAL TRIBUTE

A 'blooming' marvellous floral display, commissioned by Steam museum, has been created by Swindon Council on a roundabout in Gorse Hill, Swindon, to mark the 175th Anniversary of the Great Western Railway. The display is only yards away from the main line and will be seen by thousands of people whilst travelling by train, as well as those in cars or on foot.

The display also honours the RAF 'Wings Appeal' and, for the benefit of any 'green-fingered' enthusiasts, the flowers include, begonias, golden moss, olympia red & white and pyrethrum.   Martin Buck

The 'GREAT WESTERN INCURSION'

The Pride of Swindon
A Classic Design

Between 1927 and 1950, the GWR built six different classes of steam loco at the famous Swindon railway workshops, all based on a standard 4-6-0 design. These ranged from the 'Manor' class (a lighter version of the 'Grange') to the 'Castle' class, which handled all but the heaviest loads, these being entrusted to the 'Kings'. The 'Kings' themselves being a development of the Castle class with an even larger boiler. The six respective build details are as follows:

'Castle'	: built 1923 - 1950	Total : 171		'County'	: built 1945 - 1947	Total : 30
'Grange'	: built 1936 - 1939	Total : 80		'Hall'	: built 1928 - 1950	Total : 330
'King'	: built 1927 - 1936	Total : 30		'Manor'	: built 1938 - 1950	Total : 30

The beautiful lines of the GWR 4-6-0 class of loco is clear for all to see in this image of No.5051 'Drysllwyn Castle' (above) posing for the camera outside the old steam shed at Didcot, home of the Great Western Society. The GWR green is a stunning livery and the embellishments of cast metal nameplates and number, plus the unsparing use of brass and copper, just adds to the aesthetic nature of a Great Western steam loco. Martin Buck

---

(Previously in Loco Review)
The 'GREAT WESTERN INCURSION'

The first steam hauled charter to run in 2010 involving GWR motive power takes place on Saturday, 20th February, when two of Swindon's finest loco class' double-head a special train from Birmingham to Didcot. The details are:

Tour   : 1Z43, the 08:05 Tyseley Warwick Road - Didcot (1Z65 return)

Traction   : 'Hall' 4-6-0 No.4965 *'Rood Ashton Hall'* + 'Castle' 4-6-0 No.5043 *'Earl of Mount Edgcumbe'*

Page 216: *The morning of 20th February is bitterly cold, but sunny, and an overnight frost makes for a great exhaust display as we can see in the first two compositions. On the outward journey, No.4965 'Rood Ashton Hall' and No.5043 'Earl of Mount Edgcumbe' noisily approach the north portal of Sapperton Tunnel on the Swindon - Gloucester line after a maximum volume ascent of Sapperton Bank.* Stephen Dance

Page 217:

After a four minute stop at Swindon, the duo (top) are seen building up speed passing Highworth Junction en-route to Didcot, and another magnificent display of steam. On the return journey, with No.4965 (bottom) still leading, the train is seen on the embankment at South Marston, Swindon, travelling quite slowly back to the West Midlands. Martin Buck (2)

NAMED TRAINS

The Great Western adopted a policy of naming several passenger services on certain routes to provide a feeling of prestige, complete with a cast metal headboard placed on the smoke box door of the steam loco. Such evocative names include 'Bristolian, Red Dragon, Merchant Venturer and, perhaps, the most famous of all .... *'Cornish Riviera Express'*.

Through trains from London Paddington to Penzance started running on 1st March 1867 and fast services included the 'Cornishman' (10:15hrs departure) and 'Flying Dutchman' (11:45). However, a new express service with limited stops was introduced on 1st July 1904, leaving Paddington at 10:10hrs, conveying six carriages to Penzance, including a dining car, plus one more carriage for Falmouth, which was detached at Truro. The return train left Penzance at 10:00hrs.

A public competition in the August 1904 edition of 'Railway Magazine', was launched to choose the name for this train service and from more than 1,200 entries, two suggestions emerged, 'Cornish Riviera Limited' and 'Riviera Express', which were combined as the 'Cornish Riviera Express'.

On Saturday, 26th June, Steam Dreams run the 'Cornish Riviera Express' from London Paddington to Penzance. It features 'King Class' No.6024 'King Edward I' + 'Castle Class' No.5029 'Nunney Castle' (above) double-heading 1Z28, the 15:53 Exeter St David's - Par, leg of the tour, which is seen running through Dawlish, much to the delight of on-looking holidaymakers; Langstone Rock is prominent in the background. Richard A. Jones

(Overleaf)

Page 220: *GWR 'Castle' class 4-6-0 No.5043 'Earl of Mount Edgcumbe' (top) is in charge of 1Z43, the 13:01 Solihull - Slough, one way trip, on Friday, 16th April, to get it into position for the following day's 'Bristolian'. The first vehicle behind the tender is the new water-carrier (former Motorail van No.96175) to enable non-stop running and it looks rather good! The train is approaching Wormleighton crossing in fine style.* Geoff Plumb

Here, on the Saturday, No.5043 'Earl of Mount Edgcumbe' (bottom) hauls the 'Bristolian, running as 1Z21, the 11:33 London Paddington - Bristol Temple Meads, and is seen passing Shrivenham. For the return working, FGW and Network Rail allow the train to travel the fast road all the way from Bristol to London, giving a result of 109 minutes. Not bad going for a 1936 built loco. Only the best built at Swindon! Steven King

Page 221: *The first leg of the 'Great Britain III' grand tour sets off from London Paddington on Tuesday, 6th April, hauled by a GWR loco - 'Castle' Class No.5029 'Nunney Castle' - quite fittingly displaying '175' on the boiler door. Sadly, the occasion is marred by poor weather and No.5029 (top) is seen approaching Highworth Junction, Swindon, with 1Z27, the 12:00 Paddington - Bristol Temple Meads.* Martin Buck

Truly stunning - beauty and power in one! This special train - 'The Royal Oak' - celebrates the 80th Anniversary ('Oak') of 'King' Class 4-6-0 No.6024 'King Edward 1' entering service in 1930. In this view, No.6024 (bottom) is at the head of 1Z60, the 08:04 Paddington - Worcester, seen approaching the foot-crossing near Kingsey on Saturday, 10th July. The train is routed via High Wycombe and the return via Swindon. Geoff Plumb

The 'BRISTOLIAN'

▲ 175 - 'GREAT BRITAIN III'   **The 'ROYAL OAK' ▼**

No.3717 'City of Truro' became a record breaker when a speed of 102.30 mph was attained, whilst hauling the 'Ocean Mails' from Plymouth to London Paddington on 9th May 1904. This speed was recorded 'on board' by Charles Rous-Marten, who wrote for the 'Railway Magazine'. During the Cotswold Festival, No.3717 'City of Truro' (left) is seen taking a breather at Winchcombe before working its next train service.

Meanwhile, in this idyllic scene on the 'Honeybourne Line', Churchward / Collett 2-8-0 No.3803 (below) rounds Chicken curve on 30th May with the 11:13 Gotherington - Toddington.

Richard A. Jones (2)

GWR 175 COTSWOLD FESTIVAL of STEAM

The GWR175 Cotswold Festival of Steam runs from 29th May - 6th June at the Gloucestershire Warwickshire Railway and the event is the most ambitious the Railway has ever organised. As there are many other GWR 175 events taking place, great care has been taken to ensure the event does not clash with other planned celebrations.

To aid the celebrations, the Railway hire in other GWR locos, such as Churchward's 2-6-0 No.5322 from Didcot Railway Centre, whilst their own locos help out elsewhere; a BR Class 9F 2-10-0 at the West Somerset Railway and Churchward's 4-4-0 No.3717 'City of Truro' to both Didcot and the Swindon & Cricklade Railway.

The timetable in operation during the 10-day festival requires most trains to operate with two locos; the first of these is the one which starts a train at Toddington. The second loco is attached to the rear of the train at Winchcombe for the journey to Gotherington where, due to a previous landslip occurring beneath the run-round loop, trains run top and tail. The second loco then heads the train back to Toddington and the other loco is removed at Winchcombe.

57604

'Pendennis Castle'

This special portfolio concludes with an event to commemorate 175 years of the Great Western Railway - FGW Class 57/6 diesel loco No.57604 turned out in Great Western livery, complete with cast iron cab side number & nameplates.

Brush at Loughborough carry out the repaint, and a first rate job at that! No.57604 is unveiled to the public at Didcot Railway Centre on 20th June.

After the day's unveiling, No.57604 (top right) waits for the road at Didcot, giving the driver a chance of some last minute snaps, before a move back to Old Oak Common. It is a shame this loco will probably only be seen at night on the 'Night Riviera'.

The loco had previously been displayed (below) on the turntable at Didcot Railway Centre, to the delight of assembled cameramen.

Steven King (3)

Acknowledgements

My sincere thanks go to all the people named below who have kindly contributed images for inclusion in this edition of 'LOCO REVIEW'.. Their help, without which this book would not be possible, is much appreciated. Where applicable, I have included a note of any 'Website' address, should you wish to see more of their work.

Richard Armstrong (richardarmstrong.fotopic.net)

Ian Ball (northeastheavy.fotopic.net)

Alastair Blackwood (alastair-blackwood.fotopic.net)

Donald Cameron

Stuart Chapman

Edward Clarkson

Ian Cuthbertson (ian.mediaobject.co.uk)

Max Fowler (max-fowler.fotopic.net)

Nigel Gibbs

Stephen Dance (d1059.fotopic.net)

Richard Denny

Richard Giles

Carl Gorse (37682.fotopic.net)

Dave Gower

David Hamilton

Neil Harvey (neilharvey4789.fotopic.net)

Alan Hazelden (alan-hazelden.fotopic.net)

Mike Hemming

Guy Houston (guyhouston.fotopic.net)

Simon Howard (manorm2003.fotopic.net)

Richard A Jones (richardjones8646.fotopic.net)

Fred Kerr

Steven King (steve-king.fotopic.net)

Lee Marshall (leem.fotopic.net)

Keith McGovern

Chris Perkins (chrisperkins.fpic.co.uk)

Geoff Plumb (geoff-plumb.fotopic.net)

Kevin Poole (kevin-poole.fotopic.net)

Jim Ramsay (tayrail.fotopic.net)

Steven Robertson (aberdonianwanderers-railwayphotography.fotopic.net)

Robert Sherwood (southwestrailways.fotopic.net)

James Skoyles (railfreightcoalspictures.fotopic.net)

Nick Slocombe (trainsofthewesternworld.fotopic.net)

Jamie Squibbs (jamie7354.fotopic.net)

David Stracey

Peter Tandy (petertandy.co.uk)

Mark Thomas (mthomas.fotopic.net)

Mick Tindall

Scott Turner (scottturner2.fotopic.net)

James Welham (jameswelham.fotopic.net)

Michael Wright (37517slocopics.fotoblog.co.uk)